Peasants and Parsons

RAY BARRETT

ROBERT HALE · LONDON

ISBN 0 7090 4303 1

Robert Hale Limited
Clerkenwell House
Clerkenwell Green
London EC1R 0HT

Photoset in Garamond by
Derek Doyle & Associates, Mold, Clwyd.
Printed in Great Britain by
St Edmundsbury Press, Bury St Edmunds, Suffolk.
Bound by WBC Bookbinders Ltd, Bridgend, Glamorgan.

Contents

To the memory of
Mother and Dad

Illustrations

Cover photograph: The picture on the jacket depicts an interesting harvest scene. A shock of wheat standing head-high to Dad and Mother demonstrates the length of straw produced on newly ploughed, fertile pasture. Battered and tangled, it was too much for the little reaper and was mown off with a grass-mower, on which my brother Vic is seated, and collected into bundles. A pile of cut but ungathered corn can be seen on the right-hand side of the picture.

All photographs from the collection of the author.

Frontispiece illustration by Roger Pearce

Acknowledgements

I would like to acknowledge the help and encouragement given me by my cousin Marjorie (Miss Marjorie Poole), and also that of my daughter-in-law, Celia, who spent hours digging around in county record offices, church chests and old local newspapers for details of family history.

Some of the material in this book first appeared as articles in various magazines, and I gratefully acknowledge the publication of an article in each of the following: *Country Life* (1941), *The Countryman* (1981), *Farmers Weekly* (1981) and *Shooting Times* (1988). The sexton's reminiscences were the subject of a talk I gave on BBC Radio in 1967.

1

Through all the changing scenes of life

A century ago, cheap grain flooding in from the American prairies was helping to feed Britain's rapidly growing population, but the extremely low prices were disastrous for British growers, and angry farmers were asking, 'Who cares what happens to us?'

This book tells how one farming family set about regaining its independence and amending its fortunes after losing everything during the 'great depression' of the nineteenth century. Though the story centres round one family, such stories, it is said, are the stuff of which social history is made, and they can seldom be told without mentioning the parson from time to time along the way.

In 1871 Jim Barrett, my grandfather, was in the prime of life, thirty years old, tall, broad-shouldered, healthy and apparently happy in the belief that all was right with his world. He was then farming 135 acres of good land, mostly arable, near Banbury, and employed five men, a boy and a house servant. He led a full life, albeit an easy one, and enjoyed his ale in the convivial company of fellow farmers in their favourite hostelry in Banbury on market day. Jim, like others, failed to read the writing on the wall, though it had been written large for years, and he seemed blissfully unaware that the good days were coming to an end.

Ten years later he was farming only fifty acres with the help of one man and a boy. The end came quickly. By 1885 everything had gone, and Jim and his family were homeless. He set out to look for work as a day labourer, but, as he well knew, labourers were ten-a-penny, and work, if it could be found, was at starvation wages. It looked as though Jim, with a wife and six children to support, would be one more of the vast army already trudging from farm to farm, from village to village, in the hope of being able to earn a few shillings in spells of fine weather when outdoor work was possible. Farmers did not pay men to sit around in the barn when it was raining.

The cold truth was that farming had been going downhill ever since the repeal of the Corn Laws in 1846. The price of wheat, which had peaked at 132 shillings a quarter during the Napoleonic Wars, had slumped to 40 shillings by 1850. In a letter to the *Warwick Advertiser* dated 31 December 1849, a 'suffering tenant farmer' wrote: 'I, with many others, have been daily expecting that in these disastrous times, "The Warwickshire Agricultural Protection Society" would have been, like others, up and doing ... We should over-run the ruinous free-trade policy under whose hand we are all suffering so much. It has ruined so many honest families and prostrated so many valuable interests.' Another correspondent wrote: 'The land of this kingdom could feed and employ our population independently of any foreign supplies.'

Prices continued to fall steadily over the years until in 1885, with wheat prices down to nearly 30 shillings a quarter, Jim Barrett was finally shaken out of his complacency – and out of his farm.

The family consisted of Jim, his wife, Lizzie, Tom (my father) and five daughters. With no reasonable prospects in Britain, Jim and 12-year-old Tom set sail for Canada – at that time a land of boundless opportunities for all, or so it was said, and particularly for starving labourers and bankrupt farmers.

Meanwhile Lizzie found a home for herself and the girls in a village some fifteen miles away, near her family home, and went out cleaning and scrubbing for anyone who would employ her for a few hours a week; she also 'took in' washing, collecting and delivering up to five or six miles from home. Work was always available for girls, and the two older ones went straight into domestic service in town.

Jim, who had no money to put down on one of the cheap 'half-sections' that were going, worked on several farms in Ontario, where he and Tom discovered that, though hired hands were provided with a good meal after their day's work, living-in meant sleeping in the barn. After about two years they returned home. There was a joyful reunion with the family, and almost immediately Jim found a job on the Warwick & Napton Canal, now part of the Grand Union, and with the job went a canal-side cottage.

Jim Barrett, one-time farmer and employer of men but now at the bottom of the pile, was about to discover for himself what life was like as a labourer living in a tied cottage. Banbury market was no longer part of his world – that was for those with plenty of time and money to spend, but at the moment he had neither.

Tom, now fourteen, got a job at a local lime-works, one of several then flourishing in the area. They found employment for men from villages within walking-distance – anything up to seven or eight miles. Thanks to the lime-works, labourers in this part of Warwickshire suffered less severe hardship than did those from purely agricultural areas.

Tom walked to work along the towpath, a distance of about three miles. In winter he set off long before daybreak, and to avoid falling into the canal in the darkness would walk the entire distance with one hand outstretched so that he could feel the hedge as he went along, and so make sure that he was well away from the water's edge.

Despite the long hours, terrible working-conditions and poor pay, the men were neither depressed nor despondent. Most of them had a great sense of fun and enjoyed nothing better than a good laugh at the expense of some young, unsuspecting newcomer they were 'initiating' into the fraternity. Tom found his dinner bag full of a beautiful mixture of lime and water on several occasions, and for a week or more he was sent on a number of absolutely ridiculous errands to the foreman, who, as his experienced tormentors well knew, would be far from amused, but most of the lads were quick in the uptake and after a very short time were warmly accepted by the 'old blokes'.

Tom escaped from the lime-works when his father found him a job on the canal. He now worked outdoors all the year round, often soaked to the skin or half frozen to death, but there was more variety in the work, and he appreciated the clean, fresh air well away from the heavy pall of smoke and lung-destroying dust which perpetually enveloped the lime-works. He also picked up the rudiments of carpentry and bricklaying – skills he was to find useful in later years.

They had no transistor radio or television to entertain them as they breakfasted and prepared for work, but they did have music, even on dark winter mornings – music of a very special kind, the song of their pet blackbird. Dad told us many times that, as soon as the lamp was burning and the cover removed from the cage, the bird would burst into song. Though trapping was widely practised in those days, Tom's bird had almost certainly been taken from the nest as a fledgling and reared in captivity. That it was prepared to sing for its breakfast was proof that it was a happy, well-cared-for pet. The blackbird was always Dad's favourite songster and, in his view, superior to the nightingale, which, he maintained, was grossly overrated.

Tom spent his working hours in the company of hard-working but coarse, hard-swearing men, and he could probably have been forgiven had he allowed himself to fall to their level of grossness, though he admitted that he had always enjoyed a good earthy story or anecdote told by a real rustic raconteur, of which extrovert, 'gifted' characters there was usually at least one in every village. Unfortunately the genuine article is rarely met with these days.

Tom possessed an urge to 'improve' himself and spent most of his meagre allowance of pocket-money on books. Besides 'penny dreadfuls' and the adventures of 'Buffalo Bill' he read the *Boys' Own Paper* and *Chums*. Among his few much-loved books was a beautifully bound and illustrated *Robinson Crusoe*. He had first seen it in a shop window in Leamington, but the price put it beyond his reach. However, he saved his pennies until one day he was able to go into the shop, hand over the money and walk out with the long-coveted book in his hand. He was also fond of poetry and till late in life could quote much of 'The Village Blacksmith' by heart, but his favourite poem was Gray's 'Elegy', and while we watched some old parishioner being taken into the churchyard I have heard him say, 'The cock's shrill clarion, or the echoing horn, no more shall rouse them from their lowly bed.' I also remember his use of a 'catch-phrase' dating back to a war now all but forgotten. Towards the end of a tiring day's work, when we were aching to put away our tools and head for home, he would sometimes say, 'Don't worry. Either night or Blücher will come.'

The girls, also educated at the village school at the end of the last century, were, like Tom, fond of reading, and Mary, the oldest, began keeping a diary when she was about ten years old and kept it diligently for years after she left school.

After a spell on the canal Tom obtained the lofty position of porter at a village railway station on the LNWR branch line which ran between Leamington Spa and Rugby.

Meanwhile Jim kept steadily on at his work on the canal and was sometimes away from home for three or four days at a time. In his absence Lizzie acted as lock-keeper. She was short of stature and lightly built, but as tough as leather. With both men in regular employment and with four of her five daughters now in service, Lizzie could have settled down in her small but comfortable home, but neither she nor Jim had any intention of settling down; they had not forgotten the independence they had once enjoyed – an independence they still hoped to regain.

The road running past the cottage, though little more than a lane, was part of the old Welsh Road along which farmers had once driven their cattle to Smithfield. The road, with grass on both sides, had provided useful grazing along the way, and quiet places where the animals could be bedded down safely for the night. The journey to London was a long one, and owners took every care to ensure that cattle reached their destination in prime condition, not as worthless, limping skeletons.

The land was all enclosed when Jim arrived on the scene, but there were still wide grass verges, knee-deep with lush grass during the summer, and these Jim studied with an anticipatory gleam in his eyes. He saw possibilities there and began making plans for putting the 'long meadow', as he called it, to profitable use, but he had to move one step at a time, so one year, instead of buying a single pig to fatten for the house, he scraped together enough money to buy two: one to fatten, the other, a female, for breeding.

In due time the first sow was producing two litters a year – not for nothing was the pig regarded as 'the poor man's friend'. With the money received from the sale of weaners, he bought a heifer calf, and a second was bought as soon as possible afterwards so that the pair might grow up together. A large part of the diet of young pigs and calves consisted of skimmed milk and buttermilk, both available at almost any farmhouse door for next to nothing, especially during the summer.

Jim and Tom helped on a nearby farm during busy times, their evening and weekend work often paid for in kind – skimmed milk, chat potatoes, a few turnips or swedes, or a cart-load of straw.

Their neighbour's farm was quite large and reasonably profitable for those difficult times, but money was not wasted on inessentials. Dad said he remembered going into the large living-kitchen and being struck by the apparent lack of comfort. The flag-stoned floor, though quite clean, was quite bare except for a sack serving as hearthrug in front of the fire, while a curved piece of iron that had once been part of a cart or wagon tyre made a serviceable fender and kept the ashes together under the grate. That hard-working, frugal family prospered and moved to a bigger farm, but not many farmers' wives would have been satisfied, even in those days, with such primitive, home-made kitchen fittings.

The reward for Jim's patience and labour came the following spring, when two Shorthorn yearling heifers were taken out to graze the 'long meadow'. It was an exciting moment and a rewarding sight for both Jim and Lizzie, watching their two young, potential cows cropping the grass. From the roadside, too, they scythed grass which they made into hay for feeding the heifers through the winter.

In 1896, nearly twelve years after his downfall, Jim heard of a
small farm for sale about eight or nine miles away. The locals
knew it as 'Magpie Hall' though it was certainly no stately
home, nor did the postman know it by that name. The
farmhouse was, in fact, a 'two-up, two-down' cottage with a
thatched roof almost rotten with age, a few dilapidated farm
buildings and twenty-five acres of heavy, undrained
Warwickshire clay. Completely surrounded by fields – green
to the very door, you might say – it lay nearly a mile from a
road of any description, roughly midway between the villages
of Napton-on-the-Hill and Priors Marston and just within
the borders of the latter parish. Jim and Lizzie talked it over
for a few days and then, probably deciding that it was 'now or
never', went ahead and bought the run-down old place.

All the girls had now left school, and with both men
bringing in wages it had been possible to save a few pounds.
The older girls, in domestic service, had also saved a little and
chipped in with what they could afford. It is also possible that
Lizzie inherited a small sum of money about this time. Her
mother, my great-grandmother, who had lived at the
canal-side cottage during her last years, died there in 1895 at
the age of ninety-three. The farm was purchased in the
following year. They would also have needed money to buy a
horse and cart, essential on any farm, and one or two milking
cows to supply the household with milk and butter, and for
feeding pigs and calves.

Towards the end of that year Jim and Tom burned their
boats: they threw up their jobs and the precious wages along
with them, and shortly afterwards hitched the newly acquired
horse to a heavy, two-wheeled farm cart, loaded their
belongings on to it and, driving their few livestock ahead of
them, set off for their new home. The occasional traveller
they met along the quiet lanes probably mistook them for a
family of gypsies on the move, but that wouldn't have
worried Jim Barrett one bit.

Jim and Lizzie, both over forty when they left their
previous farm and now in their fifties, were starting again
from scratch, and while the small, remote farm they were
moving to bore no resemblance to the farm in the village
within walking-distance of the busy market town of Banbury,

both were as excited and as eager to get started as was Tom, now in his twenties. They were happy in the knowledge that they were landless labourers no longer, but farmers again.

The purchase price of the farm was £400, around £16 per acre. A deposit of £100 was paid, the balance of £300 being left on permanent mortgage, interest to be paid at a fixed rate of only four per cent per annum, an outgoing of £12 a year, roughly 50 pence an acre, and it remained at that figure until interest rates rose steeply after the end of World War II, when the mortgage was finally called in and paid off.

The £300 loan was arranged through a solicitor who had a client with money to invest. Though the price of land was low and agriculture in a depressed state, it appears that land was still considered a sound investment promising a worthwhile return to the investor.

2

Fight the good fight

Jim's first concern after settling in at the farm was to find some land on which he could grow food for his family and livestock. To have broken turf with a plough would have required a team of strong horses, something he did not possess, so, armed with a two-tined digging-fork apiece, the two men set about turning over a plot of two acres from which they hoped to gather their first harvest in due time.

But neither seasons nor crops can be hurried; they have to be awaited with patience as well as hope. Both Jim and Lizzie knew that a hard time lay ahead, but they were prepared for that. With a cow or two producing milk, and poultry and pigs supplying all the eggs and bacon they could eat, not to mention the rabbits waiting to be snared and dropped into the pot, they weren't likely to starve, and the weekly shopping-bill for other essentials was small.

Then tragedy struck. Daughter Emily, in service in Leamington, was struck down by the dreaded 'consumption' (tuberculosis) and was brought home to the farm. One day her sisters took some may-blossom into her room, but she found the heavy scent quite overpowering and asked them to take it away. The girls would certainly have known that it was considered unlucky to have may-blossom in the house but were obviously prepared to defy this ancient, deeply rooted superstition simply to see their sister's eyes light up, if only for a moment.

Emily's death at nineteen was a sad blow, but such

tragedies were almost commonplace at that time and so were of interest only to the families concerned. Her story is preserved in Mary's diary, where it is recorded in simple, poignant words.

Of the ramshackle buildings, only the small barn was made of bricks, shattered and crumbling to dust. The floor was simply dirt padded hard as concrete by the passing of many feet over the years. At one end, however, was a square of thick planks fastened down with large iron spikes. Jim instantly recognized this as the threshing-floor, though it was only just large enough to allow one man to swing a flail safely, and it was as a threshing-floor that he hoped to use it when the time came.

Decent buildings were urgently needed but would cost money. Six miles away, at Woodford Halse, on the Great Central Railway, as it then was, flourished a busy railway repair depot. In its heyday, at the turn of the century, it could house up to fifty engines, and there were large wagon-repair sheds and a turntable – all long since dismantled and silent. Here Jim bought a number of what he called 'carriage bottoms', presumably the floors of discarded railway carriages, and because they were extremely large, heavy and unwieldy they were cheap. Jim wanted them in one piece, so he hauled them home on a timber carriage hired for the purpose. Lifting and securing them in position to serve as walls for his new buildings proved rather difficult. Without any of the mechanical aids we have today, it was simply a matter of brute strength. Friends and neighbours rallied round, ensuring enough hands and enough muscle being in the right place at the right time. I believe one man was injured, though not seriously.

The first sizable cheque Jim received was for a cart-load of lambs sold at a local market – a day long remembered by the family, since it was also the first day of a new century, 1 January 1900.

The lambs had probably been born the previous March or April and would have been large and excessively over-fat by our standards. Jim favoured the giant Oxford Down breed, though this was often crossed with the Border Leicester to improve quality. Coming from a part of the country where 'close wool' breeds were folded on turnips and the like, Jim had no time for the small hill breeds – 'mountain peckers', he called them. When a neighbour pointed out to him that some of these breeds were seldom attacked by maggots, he replied, 'That's because they can run like greyhounds – no "blow fly" can catch the little devils.'

In those days, most people enjoyed a large joint of fat mutton, while for today's much more discriminating market, farmers, by some miracle of nature, have succeeded in producing nothing but fat-free, prime, lean lamb. Lambs similar to Jim's were making around 25 shillings each at the beginning of the century, a price with which he would have been satisfied.

Great care was taken of the small amount of wheat it was possible to grow, and Jim tried to put aside enough of the best grain to use as seed the following year. A change of seed was usually made by swapping a bushel or two with a neighbour. Beans, on the other hand, were grown year after year from seed produced on the farm. In a wet season the bean crop was extremely difficult to harvest and was occasionally left to rot in the field. Dad said he remembered a year when the stench of rotting beans reached and penetrated into the house over one hundred yards away. In desperation, an attempt was once made to dry the beans by placing them on trays in the oven, but the experiment was abandoned – it was like trying to drain the ocean with a bucket.

In a hot, dry season the bean pods could split open and the beans be shed on the ground unless harvested without delay, yet, in spite of all the difficulties and the risk of failure, beans were persevered with and grown as a regular and important part of crop rotation, especially on heavy ground – and Jim's was certainly heavy.

Most certainly, the sun did not always shine at harvest time. In fact, it was a succession of unusually wet harvests in the previous century which had brought many farmers already struggling, to final ruin.

The thought of hiring a threshing contractor and a gang of men to thresh out his miniature stack of corn never entered

Jim's head. He knew exactly what he had to do: he set to work and made himself a flail, using an old fork stake for the handle and a heavy piece of crab-apple wood for the business end. The old threshing-floor was about to come into its own again.

Using a flail is a pleasant, rhythmic occupation, as I learned for myself over sixty years ago, but it calls for intense concentration and a confident, easy swing of the tool. A nervous, timid swing or a momentary lapse of concentration is certain to result in a painful crack on the head. Consequently the art, or knack, of using a flail was learned quickly or not at all. Nevertheless, once the knack has been acquired, the work, though not as easy as it looks, is deeply satisfying.

The well-worn, home made flail hung in its accustomed place on a large nail in the barn for years after it was last used, somewhere around the mid 1920s. It is now, I believe, an exhibit in a farm museum somewhere in Warwickshire. Any visitors who deign to give it a passing glance as they stroll round, most of them looking bored to death, could be forgiven for seeing nothing more than an inanimate, not very interesting, primitive hand tool, while I, seeing it through very different eyes, would see a weather-beaten man in shirt-sleeves rhythmically thumping the ears of corn spread on the barn floor before him – corn needed to provide his family with bread.

Fortunately it is now being recognized that a farm museum, if it is to be of lasting interest and value, needs to be a 'working museum', not simply a display of lifeless 'exhibits'.

For separating the wheat from the chaff, a winnowing-machine was needed. Luckily, Jim was able to buy one locally for a few shillings, and he and Tom spent many a winter afternoon threshing and winnowing in the barn, where working-conditions were reasonably comfortable even in very cold weather. The winnowing-machine was little more than a large box about the height of a piano, about two foot wide and open at one end. A large fan at the closed end blew out the chaff at the other end while a set of oscillating riddles removed other rubbish. Fan and riddles were operated by turning a handle. It was quite fascinating to watch, though there was nothing 'hi-tech' about it, but it did a very satisfactory job and left the corn clean enough to go to the mill to be ground into flour.

Hay and corn harvest were family operations on all but the largest farms. Lizzie's task in the harvest field, whenever she had time to spare, was to lay bonds (a handful of corn stakes with ears all at one end with which she tied up the sheaves) while the men slogged away with fagging-hooks and sticks. In slack moments she would give a hand with the reaping, using the primitive sickle in preference to the hook and stick. The reaping-hook, or fagging-hook as we called it, has changed little over the years and is still used by gardeners and others for chopping down long grass and tall weeds. The stick, which resembled a large 'tick', was from two to three feet long with a sharp-angled crook at one end. With the hook in one hand and the stick in the other the reaper was able to gather the corn into sheaves lift them around and place them on the bonds. Using a sickle calls for little skill or muscle power, but it is slow, back-breaking work, and the user can be sure of suffering a blistered hand in no time at all. The operator grasps a handful of standing corn in one hand, puts the sickle behind and cuts through with a sawing action, making use of the tool's serrated edge, at the same time pulling the sickle towards him. An experienced hand would swipe off the handful of corn in one easy movement.

When any of the girls – now all grown up – were on holiday at the farm, they loved nothing better than lending a hand in the harvest field. The older ones had helped with the harvest on the farm near Banbury when they were children, and Mary recorded in her diary in the summer of 1878, when she was eleven years old, that on a certain date the school broke up for the 'harvest holidays'.

Mary's reference conjures up a picture of an almost deserted village, the women and children out in the fields laying bonds for the men or, with the farmer's permission, gleaning stray ears of corn to be threshed and ground into flour for household use and, when it could be spared, to enrich the diet of the precious family pig. Only the all-important harvest could justify a five- or six-week shut-down of the school – every child's help was needed in the field to ensure that as much as possible was safely gathered in. Nor had things changed much since then, and Lizzie went carefully over every square yard of ground in search of any ears that had escaped being collected into the sheaves – corn was still much too valuable to be left lying around for the pigeons.

When Jim was able to afford a much-needed second horse, he became the proud owner of a 'pair', Lion and Blossom, and though he was well aware of their limitations on his heavy land, he decided to double his arable acreage, from two acres to four. With wheat making only 30 shillings a quarter, he had no intention of launching out as an arable farmer again; he simply wanted to grow as much as possible of his own stockfeed and have flour in the bin for breadmaking. He also found that, with so much arable land still going down to grass, straw was becoming scarce and dear. It was in demand for bedding, for supplementing hay as winter fodder and for thatching. Jim saw no sense in paying good money for what he knew he could grow on the farm.

Another reason for ploughing more land was that he intended making a fallow of about a third of his arable acreage each year, as a means of keeping his crops clean and his land workable. So, with the help of his neighbour, two more acres of turf were ploughed. Although the fallow was then considered an essential part of good husbandry, it is now dismissed as uneconomic and unnecessary, unless the new-fangled idea of 'set-aside' is regarded as a fallow. To be paid for resting land while it builds up fertility, enabling it to produce bumper crops in the future must indeed be money for old rope.

Jim's first crops were weakly and yields disappointing, and it was obvious that the field badly needed draining, so he decided to drain it. He and Tom took their spades and dug a number of trenches with outfalls into a ditch, and in the trenches they laid clay tile pipes hauled from the brickworks at Napton. They possessed no surveyor's instruments – only a 'good eye'; nevertheless, most of those drains were still working satisfactorily thirty years later.

Still lying around after I left school in the early 1920s were a couple of rather tattered corn sacks bearing Jim's name and address in three-inch, well-stencilled, bright red letters. They were the remnant of half a dozen purchased in the early years of the century and were three-bushel sacks then in common use along with the four-bushel, half-quarter sack. When a young man could run up the granary steps with a full sack of either size on his back, he could claim to have reached the noble state of manhood.

Jim was not being extravagant or vain when he paid out good money on those sacks – he was merely being sensible. Along with other farmers, he took his corn to be ground at the local mill, but he wasn't always satisfied with the result and suspected that the flour he collected from the mill was sometimes not his own. It was difficult to identify plain, unmarked sacks with certainty, and although 'personal' sacks were no guarantee against substitution or pilfering of either corn or flour, their owners believed they were less likely to be tampered with. Jim was simply taking precautions, although it is possible that, having married a miller's daughter, he had acquired a suspicious mind.

Farmers and cottagers alike were dependent on their pig for several months' supply of meat during the winter, and on well-cured bacon and ham for most of the year. The loss of a pig, especially after having fed it for three or four months, could be a disaster for a poor family. To alleviate distress when such a calamity occurred, mutual help societies were formed in many parishes, into which members paid a small weekly subscription. The funds raised paid for the replacement of a pig that had died or the feeding of one for a family that had fallen on hard times as a result of sickness or unemployment.

Before the outbreak of the First World War, Napton, with a population of nearly a thousand, had a flourishing pig club known as 'The Napton Pig Assurance Association', with a membership of sixty-six. At the club's annual meeting and supper at the King's Head in 1912, a letter of apology for his absence was received from the vicar, along with 5 shillings and instructions that the money was 'to be spent during the evening among those present'. Free of Parson John's inhibiting presence but with his money to spend, a very pleasant evening was assured.

Those were busy days for the local pig-killer, though his services were never called upon at Magpie Hall. Jim did his own slaughtering and butchering, self-taught, no doubt, at the expense of his first unsuspecting victims. At the killing, Lizzie stood with a jug to catch the blood as it pumped from the dying animal's throat. She believed in making her black puddings with blood fresh from its source. The curing of the bacon was also her responsibility, a skill handed down from one generation to the next.

The downfall of some farmers during the long years of depression was attributed to the expensive habits and tastes of their wives. They were women who prided themselves on being ladies of fashion. One local farmer's wife boasted quite openly that she dressed much better than her neighbours' wives, who, she said, had no dress-sense whatever. When her husband went bankrupt, she berated him for an incompetent fool. His neighbours shook their heads and also called him a fool.

But Lizzie was not of that breed. Her only break from the daily grind was an hour in chapel on a Sunday evening, mostly during the summer, when walking across the fields in long skirts was not too difficult. Jim would sometimes meet her after the service, but had he accompanied her to the very door of either chapel or church she would not have succeeded in getting him across the threshold.

The village of Priors Marston, with a population of around 400, boasted three Nonconformist chapels – Moravian, Wesleyan Methodist and Primitive Methodist, Lizzie's usual place of worship. Though the Methodist chapels have been converted into dwellings, the Moravian church is still active. The preponderance of chapel folk prompted Jim to say, 'Don't bury me among that lot of long-eared ranters.' He and Tom stayed at home on Sundays, well assured that they were getting along quite nicely without chapel, church or parson.

Contact with the Church of England was made when a young man from Leamington, courting one of the daughters, took her to the parish church occasionally on a Sunday evening. After seeing her home after the service he set out and walked the twelve miles back to Leamington – all for love.

Tom, though he attended no place of worship, was not quite the hard-bitten 'heathen' his father was and, remembering being taken to chapel when he was a boy, never forgot the lively hymns they used to sing. In fact, he bought himself an American organ and with the aid of an instruction manuel, taught himself to play a few of his favourite 'Moody and Sankey' sacred songs.

The yearning for music is deep and universal. At the big houses a daughter would relieve the boredom of a long winter evening by playing on the pianoforte with soft, delicate fingers. But labourers, too, with less delicate fingers, loved making music and proudly played their stringed instruments in church on Sunday, while others, equally unlettered, along with a few boys, formed the choir.

The church of St Lawrence, Napton-on-the-Hill, like many others, once had its singers' or musicians' gallery across the back of the church from which players and singers manifested their skill. I remember seeing a cello standing in the parlour in the house of one of Mother's relations and was told that a member of the family had once played it in the gallery at church, aided and abetted by two or three other fiddle-players.

After the installation of the organ, practice could take place only in church, a cold, draughty, inhospitable place on a winter's night. With portable instruments it was possible to practise round a good fire at the home of one of the musicians or singers. If a barrel of beer or a bottle or two of home-made wine were available, choir practice could be quite an enjoyable occasion.

The organ put an end to all that and left a lot of people feeling unwanted, but history repeats itself, and today's parson, having decided that 'people participation' is now the name of the game, has brought back musicians and singers. Boys and girls in bum-tight jeans stand on the chancel steps, strum guitars and sing, and all the people clap their hands.

3

Those who love and those who labour

It took Jim nine or ten years to get his holding fully stocked – building up stock numbers by breeding is a slow business. Nevertheless, the day arrived when he found himself in need of more acres. He had been keeping an eye on some adjoining glebe land for some time but had calculated that there was no need to go running after it, nor did he have to wait too long before the landlord, the vicar of Napton-on-the-Hill, turned up at the farm with the information that he had thirty acres of glebe to let conveniently adjoining Jim's farm, and that if he were interested he could have it at a rent of £1 an acre per annum. The rents from the church lands, or glebe, provided the parson's living, and unless he were a man of independent means, unlet acres seriously reduced his income. Like most landlords, he was in no position to dictate terms, and a rent of 15 shillings was finally agreed. He probably considered himself lucky to have found a tenant – he certainly had no intention of farming his own glebe in those difficult times.

The thirty acres of land which ran alongside the farm consisted of two fields of neglected, tumble-down arable which had produced nothing but weeds for several years. Even so, it increased Jim's acreage from twenty-five acres to fifty-five. The land was poor, and the fences were in a bad state, but landlords were usually prepared to supply fencing-materials on the understanding that tenants carried out the work, an arrangement which proved satisfactory for many years.

The two men were busy repairing fences one day when they were surprised to see the vicar's gardener pushing a wheelbarrow in their direction. He said he'd been sent to collect the fencing left-overs – off-cuts, broken rails, chips or shavings – indeed, anything likely to burn on the vicarage fires. Jim could hardly believe that Parson John would send an old man a mile across fields for a few scraps of wood; fencing waste was generally regarded as a tenant's perk, anyhow, and the parson would have known that. Jim lost no time in informing his visitor that the stuff would burn as well on his own fire as on the parson's, and the old man left, his wheelbarrow as empty as when he came. It was no business of Jim's to know that the large vicarage was a cold barn of a place and that perhaps the parson's need of fuel was even greater than his own.

The fifty-five acres kept both men fully occupied, and Jim, now turned sixty, had no ambition to extend his boundaries further. He and Lizzie had achieved what they had set out to do – to retrieve their pride by regaining independence. There was a little money in the bank, they could look every tradesman in the eye, and they could sleep at night.

A few haymaking implements were acquired during the early years of the century. Besides cutting out some of the hard work, they also helped to speed things up quite a bit; and the purchase of a large butter churn and a cream separator was an exciting step forward, bringing to an end the need to 'set' the milk in pans after every milking and to skim off the cream by hand after it had 'risen'.

The sale of butter brought in a small weekly income, though it varied considerably, the price fluctuating from a shilling a pound during the glut months of the summer to around half a crown in winter, when it became extremely scarce. The poor quality of the cows' diet also affected the quality of the butter: it was pale in colour, with a rancid smell, and not very palatable.

Though the family were still far from rich, their fortunes had improved sufficiently to allow Tom to take a wife at the age of thirty-six, no great age for a farmer's son to marry.

It was on his weekly trip to Napton with butter and eggs that Tom met Maggie, the carrier's daughter, his senior by one year. Her family, too, were struggling to make a living off a few acres of land but were enterprising enough to go out and augment their income with a carrier's business – a twice-weekly run to Leamington Spa, a round journey of about twenty miles which took up most of the day.

Maggie, strong and independent, had taken a post as children's nurse in London when she was only sixteen (in 1888) and often used to tell us about the hustle and bustle of the crowds at busy Clapham Junction and about wheeling her charges around the common of an afternoon. She returned home a few years later to 'keep house' for her widowed father.

Just how quickly romance blossomed I could never discover – people were so reticent about such things in those days. It is more than possible that they indulged in a little kissing in the moonlight, even at their age, but it's doubtful whether they were ever caught rolling in the hay. I know Mother was as proud of her engagement ring as any young bride-to-be and that the two were married in Napton parish church in June 1909. They set up house in a small cottage on the edge of the village, from which Tom walked across the fields every day to the farm.

A few months later, a 2-year-old, unbroken Welsh cob was bought, and after it had been 'broken', a smart dog-cart and dazzling new set of driving harness appeared – the whole turn-out being a joint wedding present from the two families. A pony and dog-cart was something of a status symbol – it put its owner a step or two up the social ladder, a rung or two nearer the Joneses.

Kitty, a lovely, misty roan, was an active little filly, always impatient and straining to dash off at a smart trot. She served the family faithfully for twenty-five years and when she died was not replaced.

About a year after her marriage Maggie was driving through the village at her usual spanking pace when, turning a corner much too sharply, she was thrown out of the trap.

Neither Maggie nor pony was seriously hurt, but I was born shortly afterwards, in October 1910, though I wasn't expected until December. Such a puny little creature I was, at 3½ pounds, that many who peeped at me shook their heads ruefully and said, 'You'll never rear him.'

Tom, the proud father, would not accept the possibility that he might lose his first-born son and heir, little squeaker though he was. In later years he used to tell us how, in addition to Mother's all-out efforts to sustain me, he would try me with drops of milk from a spoon, a method he often used to ensure that a cold, weakly lamb took nourishment when too far gone to suck its mother's teat or a bottle. Then one day he noticed my eyes, wide-open for the first time, following the flight of a crow passing overhead. This splendid achievement of mine assured him that the battle for my survival had been won.

In 1913 Jim and Lizzie, both now around seventy, decided to call it a day. So it was that Tom and Maggie, with two children, for I now had a baby sister, moved to the farm while Jim and Lizzie moved to the cottage. Still very active, they maintained a keen interest in the farm which continued to provide both families with a modest living. A bonus was Mr Lloyd George's Old Age Pension of five shillings a week which Jim collected from the Post Office. (Though Mr Lloyd George received much acclaim and his name has always been coupled with its introduction, the government of the day was under the premiership of Mr H. Asquith).

About this time their daughter Mary was able to buy the cottage, thus ensuring them an even greater degree of independence, and allowing them to live out their days in reasonable comfort, their wants never exceeding their needs.

Jim died at the age of eighty-five, while Lizzie, despite the hard life she had lived, reached the ripe age of ninety, while the cottage, the little house where I was born, passed out of the family's hands when it was sold off about ten years ago.

Though a second generation was now installed at Magpie Hall and was settling down to the grim task of wresting a living from its unkind soil, life went on very much as before. The great difference was that Tom and Maggie were not starting from scratch. The farm was now stocked, butter and eggs were bringing in a small but regular income, the arable was yielding its harvest, and they had a pair of strong working horses, not to mention the pony and trap in which they could trot into town like a couple of toffs whenever they had an hour to spare.

Nevertheless, farming prospects were far from rosy, and the going would be tough. Prices and wages, still depressed, were very much as they had been within living memory. More wheat than ever was coming from North America, beef was coming from South America, while from across the Channel the French had been sending eggs for years. In fact, I have in front of me the price of eggs sold at Leadenhall Market in January 1860. English eggs were selling at 15 shillings per case of 120, and French eggs at 12 shillings per case. In July of the same year English eggs were making 8s.6d. to 10 shillings per case of one hundred, while French eggs could be bought for 8 shillings.

Tom, after working so long at his father's side, missed his companionship and his guidance, for Jim, like most farmers of his day, had kept a tight hand on the reins, allowing Tom little opportunity of gaining business experience or of taking any responsibility; it had been no part of Tom's job to make decisions. Almost overnight, all that changed.

Fortunately he had found a partner on whom he could depend for all the support he might need.

Mother having put on the mantle Lizzie had laid aside. She was made of the same stuff as her mother-in-law, so Tom had found the perfect partner, one prepared to share and take an active part in a way of life promising little but long hours and grinding toil. She was as ready and as able to chop wood, haul water from the well or wield a hayfork as she was to cook a meal, cure bacon or ply a needle, yet always on hand to give the children the care they needed.

Tom soon discovered that he had married an enterprising young lady. One winter, soon after taking over as mistress at the farm, she kept twenty-one pullets in the barn and succeeded in keeping most of them in lay throughout the winter. They were kept indoors day and night, with plenty of straw to scratch around in, and were fed a warm, wet mash in the

morning, made principally of sharps, (ground wheat offal) to
which a teaspoonful of the magic 'Karswood Poultry Spice'
was added, giving it a pleasant, appetizing aroma. In the
afternoon a good feed of whole grain, wheat or maize, sent
the birds to roost with full crops.

Free-range poultry produce few eggs during the winter, as
most of the food they consume is used to maintain body heat,
so Maggie's pullets were turning out eggs when supplies were
scarce and prices high and at the time of year when income
from butter sales was at its lowest level. Her success was
achieved without spending a penny on artificial heat or light,
while at the same time her flock was safely secured against
prowling foxes. Maggie was a pioneer in the deep-litter
system of poultry-keeping.

After harvest, the poultry, in small, portable 'stubble
houses', were taken into the field and given the pleasure of
cleaning up any grain still lying in the stubble, though they
were in competition with pigeons and a host of other birds.

Dad returned from the village one afternoon in August 1914
and burst into the living-room excitedly waving a newspaper.
That it contained startling news was obvious, even to me.
That copy of the *Daily Chronicle* had brought us news of the
outbreak of war. Conversation at meal-times from then on
included a number of words I'd never heard before, and a
few, such as 'Kaiser' and 'Zeppelin', sounded quite alarming
and stuck in my mind.

On 1 November an event occurred which disrupted the
routine of life in the household. Mother was in bed, though
we weren't told why, and a woman I'd never set eyes on
before arrived and said she had come to look after us. Though
it was long past our bedtime, we did not go to bed. Later still,
Dad came in with a strange man who hurried straight
upstairs. Dad had driven the pony and trap to Napton to
collect the doctor, who, though he doubtless had a pony and
trap of his own, would never have found his way across the
fields and through the muddy gateways in the dark.

The woman who acted as replacement mother and general
housekeeper probably served as midwife and nurse also, since
no other woman came near us. Janet was probably one of

those extremely useful members of the community who were willing and able to tackle anything, from assisting at a birth to 'laying out' a corpse. She was neither old nor ugly as so many such fictional characters are but was, in fact, a very pleasant, youngish person, and my sister and I took to her from the start.

The arrival of the young brother who had been the cause of all the fuss brought about a change in our sleeping-arrangements. Baby Vic proved to be a cuckoo in the nest. He took possession of my sister's cot, she was moved into my bed, and a pallet was laid for me on the floor in the corner of the bedroom in which we all slept. With the idea of making my sleeping-place look more like a bed, Dad took the front board of an old float, complete with some prettily shaped metalwork designed to support the reins, and screwed it to the bedroom floor. It made quite an attractive footboard, though I suppose it must have looked a little strange and somewhat out of place in a bedroom. Nevertheless, I'm sure I slept as soundly as I would in the most luxurious of beds.

Southam, a small town about five miles away, was the nearest business centre. It boasted two banks, a firm of solicitors and a number of shops, though I best remember it for the strange smell which always hung over the place – the not-unpleasant smell betraying the presence of the small gasworks which then served the town.

On one visit to the town Mother and I sat in the trap waiting for Dad when I suddenly felt most uncomfortable and badly wanted to relieve myself. Wriggling about in some distress at Mother's side, I told her I couldn't possibly wait till we got home. There were no public toilets in Southam in those days but Mother directed me to a yard with some buildings in it. In the yard, which I found without any trouble, two men were busy harnessing a pony, and apparently guessing the reason for my presence in their yard one of the men pointed to a nearby building.

I opened the door and stepped inside. For a moment, after leaving bright sunlight, it seemed almost dark in there, and before I had taken a couple of steps I stumbled over something. My eyes quickly became accustomed to the light, and I could see, not more than a foot in front of my face, the head of a beast. I remember most vividly the long horns attached to it. I was old enough to realize that the two men in the yard were butchers and that they had sent me into the slaughterhouse. I was badly shocked and for a moment froze stiff with terror, but I didn't scream and dash out. I shut my eyes, did what I had gone there to do and walked out. If those men were hoping to get a good laugh when the little boy came screaming out, they were disappointed. I suppose they should have known better than to have sent me in there, though it was possibly only thoughtlessness on their part.

Feeling rather shaky but tight-lipped and silent, I got back to the trap, clambered in and sat at Mother's side till Dad returned. I didn't say a word about what I had seen in that yard, nor did either of my parents appear to notice anything amiss with me. I don't know why I kept it all bottled up when I was probably dying to confide in someone, but I suppose I was afraid of being called a baby or a coward. For some inexplicable reason I have never breathed a word about it until today.

On leaving Southam we sometimes called in at the gasworks, where an empty drum holding perhaps four or five gallons was taken from the back of the trap and filled with tar. Dad swore by it as a preservative and gave the corrugated iron roofs of the farm buildings and the wooden walls a good coating every few years.

In Southam, too, was a chemist who did a good trade with farmers. A knowledgeable man about all things agricultural and veterinary, he would quickly make up a drench and give instructions on dosing the animal. Dad sometimes went to him for a bottle of laudanum for drenching a sick animal. The shop also stocked a wide variety of agricultural sundries, including sheep-dip, rat poison and blue vitriol (sulphate of copper) for dressing seed corn against disease. Surprising though it may sound, it was also possible to buy butter-colouring. It was used by some farmers' wives during the winter when the butter would otherwise have been as colourless as lard. Mother was no exception, for she, like all vendors of food, liked her produce to look attractive and pleasing to the eye.

All things bright and beautiful

One warm, spring afternoon soon after our arrival at the farm I made my first venture across the cow-yard and found myself in the home paddock. There I came upon an amazing sight and for a moment or two stood gazing at it, wide-eyed with wonder. A beautiful white carpet of starry-eyed daisies was spread before me and seemed to cover the entire field. Though I was not more than 3½ years old at the time I have never forgotten that first breathtaking glimpse of Nature's wonderland, but neither shall I ever forget coming face to face with the opposite side of that beautiful picture.

It happened when I discovered Dad, skinning, or cutting up, the carcase of a sheep, a knife in his hand and blood on his arm. I didn't understand what he was doing but I know I was absolutely terrified and ran, sobbing, into the house to Mother. It was a frightening experience, but this is how country children, sensitive and insensitive alike, begin to learn at an early age that life and death, beauty and ugliness are inseparable, and that out of this year's death and decay next year's flowers will bloom, to delight us with their fragrance and beauty. At that time I had no idea that the warm, woolly rug beside my bed on which I knelt each night to say my prayers had, not so long since, been walking round the fields on a sheep's back.

The grisly, discoloured carcase of a skinned sheep often hung from the branch of a tree in the orchard, high enough to be out of the reach of dogs and foxes. From it Dad would hack of chunks to feed to pigs and poultry. Bones, sheep's skulls and other revolting objects could be seen lying around the yard almost all the year round. When the remains of a carcase were buried, they weren't put into a hole in the ground at a decent depth but thrown on the muckle, the manure heap, and covered with a few forkfuls of muck – and usually uncovered by dogs before many hours had passed. Though Dad and his contemporaries had yet to learn about hygiene, they certainly knew the value of decomposed flesh and saw to it that none was wasted. Theirs was an unsavoury method of practising organic farming. After muck-spreading, stones and other objects likely to damage the mowing-machine were collected up, and there was usually a good assortment of bones which were put aside for the first 'rag and bone man' who happened along.

Farming was still in a very bad way in 1914, but workmen were secretly building submarines in German shipyards, and when these were let loose upon the high seas, the flood of cheap imported food gradually dried up and farmers suddenly found themselves making money. In 1914 wheat was fetching around 35 shillings a quarter; by the following year it had leaped to 53 shillings, and the price of bread doubled, from 4 pence to 9 pence for a four-pound loaf. This caused a great public outcry, and price controls were introduced. The price of bread was stabilized at 9 pence a loaf.

At least one windmill and an engine-driven mill were operating within a few miles of the farm, so Dad, like his father before him, took his corn to the mill, the engine-driven mill on the outskirts of Priors Marston, in which parish we lived, being the nearest, and he sometimes took me along with him. During the winter, deep ruts awash with water and of varying depth caused the cart to lurch from side to side alarmingly, and for my safety I was made to crouch in the bed of the cart among the sacks. Even there I didn't feel safe, and every now and then I was sure the cart was about to overturn. Lion sometimes had his work cut out to heave the cart out of a boggy patch onto firmer ground. Those large, cumbersome wheels might look ridiculous to us but they were designed for the work they had to do.

As the war progressed, the demand for horses rose dramatically, and so did prices. Besides being vitally important for farm work – food production depended entirely on horse power – and for every form of transport, horses were needed by the army – as many as it could lay its hands on. Losses were frightfully heavy on the battlefields of Europe, and numbers were seriously depleted, but it's an ill wind ... Dad jumped aboard the wagon and bred from Blossom and Kitty. At the same time, hay, especially of horse-feeding quality, became an extremely valuable commodity, and a farmer with a rick, or half a rick, to sell could pick up a useful cheque. The old maxim that a rick of hay standing over till the following year was as 'good as money in the bank' was forgotten during the profitable war years. It was a time for cashing in on anything saleable.

Farm prices rose steeply during the years 1915 – 19. Wheat, which had averaged 35 shillings a quarter in 1914, had risen to 53 shillings by 1918, and of course, all other prices rose too. Before the war, dairy cows were selling at prices ranging from £10 to £16 each, according to quality, but at a farm sale in the village in 1918 good cows made over £40. At the same sale, three horses made over 140 guineas apiece; before the war such horses could have been picked up for £30 or less; shire horses of good parentage were making over 200 guineas. These high prices indicate the vital role of the horse for the production of food on the farms, for the transport of guns and supplies to the battlefield and for every form of transport at home – the butcher, the baker and the undertaker needed a horse.

An exciting family upheaval occurred in June 1916. In that month we left the cottage and moved to a big house in Napton so that I could go to school, being now 5½ years old. The house, a long, stone building stood in about three acres of land made up of a pony paddock with a fascinating stream at the bottom, the delight of any boy, an orchard and a very large garden. The rent was £20 per annum. At the same time Dad also obtained the tenancy of a sixteen-acre pasture field conveniently situated on the roadside near his new home, bringing his holding to a little over seventy acres. The rent was £3 per acre, but for good feeding pasture such a figure was not unusual in some parts of Warwickshire even in the lean years before the outbreak of World War I.

Although I was nearly six years old when I started school, I was told that I was not too far behind the other children of my age, probably because my parents had done their best to give me a good start in reading and, for some reason best known to themselves, had also taught me to tell the time. Nevertheless, having been a bit of a loner, free to roam the fields on my own, to gather flowers to watch the antics of the birds, I know it was several weeks before I settled down to school life.

On our way to and from school we passed the blacksmith's shop, and though the smith might not have started work when we passed in the morning, there was often a horse or two tied at the gate patiently awaiting his arrival. The shop had a great fascination for most of us, and after afternoon school we would gather round the open door to watch the round-shouldered man at work. Each time he thrust a partially made horseshoe deep into the glowing embers in the forge and pumped the bellows, the fire would quickly glow white-hot and a shower of bright sparks would light up the gloomy interior of the shop for a moment or two, especially at dusk on a winter afternoon.

Besides being very round-shouldered, Harry suffered from a cleft palate, making his speech almost unintelligible at times, and he had an explosive temper. But in good mood or bad and despite his speech handicap, from the tone of his voice and wild gesticulations both horse and man found little difficulty in getting his drift.

If a fidgety horse had tried his short temper, he would pummel it with the hammer in his hand and, still waving the hammer around, would then shout at us to 'bugger off'. If, by some miracle, he chanced to be in a reasonably good mood, he might gruffly order one of us to put a hand to the bellows and not 'stand there doin' nothin'. Unfortunately, most of us were too small to reach the handle and could only look on enviously while the bigger boys tried their hardest to keep the bellows full – it usually took two to do it.

I half-expect to see the old place each time I pass through

the village, but the wind of change has passed over it, and it is gone.

My lingerings at the smithy door came to an end when I moved from the infants' school to the boys' at about eight years of age. My new school, situated in another part of the village, was a simple, rectangular stone building with a small lobby fitted with coat-hooks tacked on one end. Lengthwise, it stood parallel with the road and only a few feet from it which was probably the reason why there were no windows on that side. The road served as playground. Although no partition divided the room, the staff of two, their desks at opposite ends of the building, were able to control and teach their classes without having to shout each other down. The village's three schools employed a staff of six, the only man teaching the senior boys.

The boys' school was a 'National' school (National Society for Promoting Religious Education in Schools in Accordance with the Principles of the Church of England) but, though closely associated with the church, enjoyed a degree of independence, having its own board of managers who would have resented interference from the parson, who, though he visited the school occasionally, did not 'examine' the pupils.

The school lacked the luxury of a piano, although the infants' and girls' school each had one. The managers and others who had the welfare of the boys so much at heart probably believed that music was a refinement unlikely to be of benefit to a bunch of thick-headed bumpkins, most of whom would be working on a farm or in a quarry as soon as possible after reaching the age of fourteen. But the 'Boss', as he was known, did not share that view. In fact, the boys who sang in the church choir received much of their training from him, though he was not choirmaster nor, indeed, a regular worshipper at the church.

In 1893 the choir had numbered eight men and nine boys, and it remained at about that strength until the First World War. Just before the outbreak of war the local paper reported that, 'The choir rendered an anthem at morning and evening service on Easter Day.'

Lacking a piano, the 'Boss' resorted to a tuning-fork and

taught the tonic sol-fa notation – probably a good method of teaching 'pitch'. He was always impeccably dressed in a well-cut, light grey suit, and neither tie nor jacket was removed on the hottest summer afternoon. He obviously believed that such things were important, although most of his pupils were poorly dressed labourers' sons.

Very few boys left his school unable to read and write, and he did his best to stimulate an interest in reading. Eighteen- and 20-year-old quarry workers were avid readers of 'Buffalo Bill' and 'Sexton Blake' stories – apparently the Boss's efforts succeeded in planting in his pupils the seeds of a habit which continued to grow long after they had left school, a habit from which they obviously derived a great deal of pleasure. Besides lessons set apart for 'silent reading' from books in his small library, he also read aloud to us, sitting on the corner of his desk, one leg dangling; and I recall most vividly his reading of R.M. Ballantyne's *Coral Island*. The eagerly awaited 'next instalment' probably stimulated us to read for ourselves.

His neatly trimmed goatee beard was sometimes a source of amusement to both old and young, yet he left an enduring mark on his boys and on the village.

As the war progressed, food for man and beast became increasingly scarce. More wheat was urgently needed, and Dad, along with his neighbours, was called upon to do his bit and was ordered to plough up the remainder of the field containing his plot of arable. The task of breaking the turf was far beyond the capabilities of Lion and Blossom, but there was a war on and the government came to the rescue.

A pair of steam-engines was expected which would haul a large plough backwards and forwards across the field on a cable, keeping a man busy all day carting coal and water to satisfy their ravenous hunger and insatiable thirst. Instead, a tractor and plough arrived.

On Saturday morning I went along to the field, hoping to see this wonderful machine at work. A group of three or four men wearing khaki overcoats reaching down to their ankles was standing round the tractor but didn't appear to be doing much. What and who they were, I never discovered. They said they had been trying for ages to get it started, but not a 'splutter' had they been able to get out of it. When rain began to fall steadily, the men packed up their tools and left. I believe the tractor was known as a 'Titan', but whatever its name, I never saw it plough a single furrow.

The field was eventually ploughed without any assistance, though I'm sure I heard Dad telling Mother that 'they' hadn't made a very good job of it; a good team of horses would have done better. Nevertheless, it was scuffled and harrowed and sown with wheat for the next year's harvest.

Dad's extra acres, sown with wheat, eventually produced a crop, but harvesting it presented considerable difficulty. Having no binder, there was nothing for it but the fagging-hook and, inevitably, long, weary hours of back-breaking work. However, despite the field's being so far from the village, one or two horny-handed quarry labourers turned up in the evenings and on Saturday afternoons to give a hand, and their help made all the difference. In fine weather work was possible until after darkness had fallen, though the sheaves became much heavier after sunset, when dew-drenched bindweed and green thistles, heavy with sap, were pulled into the sheaves and tied up with the corn.

Such crops needed to stand in the field for a week or two, but few farmers possessed the necessary patience and faith, and corn was usually carted as soon as the sheaves were fairly slack in their bonds, an indication that the contents had wilted to some extent.

The corn was carted to the village to be threshed. A farmer allowed a number of his smaller neighbours to stack their corn in or near his rickyard, and they, in return, helped him when he needed to muster a gang to thresh his own larger ricks. Mutual help was essential when so many men were at 'the front', and prisoners of war were not always available. Under this arrangement the farmer was sure of having a threshing gang on hand whenever he needed one.

Many allotment holders grew a quarter or half an acre of wheat or barley for their pigs or poultry, and they brought their harvest and stacked it near the others. It sometimes took the crops from three or four allotments to make a worthwhile stack, large enough to provide a full day's work for the threshing contractor. When one man had made his contribution to the stack, a layer of threshed straw was spread thinly over it before the next man's was added, thus ensuring that each received his own when it came to be threshed.

The allotment also provided that other staple food and appetite-stayer, the potato. I remember passing a cottage one evening just as the man was returning from his day's work in the quarry, covered from head to foot with clay. He spotted his children playing in the road and shouted, 'Now, you lot. Get up on that 'lotment and start knocking them bloody clats [clods] about.'

Clay soil, if recently dug, dried hard in the spring and was difficult to break down to a tilth. 'Weathering' was the only satisfactory tilth-maker, but in late spring this was not possible and the large clods usually dried as hard as concrete. This man's patch of ground, probably intended for potatoes, could be worked down only the hard way, and every member of the family capable of handling a tool of some kind was expected to help.

During potato planting and harvesting, as well as in corn harvest, a man would sometimes go straight from his work to the allotment, where his wife and children would meet him with food and drink. After a short break it was all hands to the wheel till darkness fell. In busy times play was a luxury for most children but at others a variety of games were played and much enjoyed, simple though most of them were.

The arrival of spring was always most welcome. In March the mud on the untarred roads dried up and was blown away in clouds of dust by the strong winds, leaving the roads looking white and clean. Then out came the spinning tops, the hoops and the marbles. The girls marked out squares which they numbered and over which they played hop-scotch, sometimes with a piece of stone or tile, sometimes with a ball. The boys enjoyed playing tip-cat, once a very popular game in which a short, pointed stick placed on the ground is struck near the tip with another longer stick and made to rise into the air when it is given a good swipe with the longer stick. The object, to drive the cat as far as possible. Though after a pig-killing they were able to indulge in the more robust game of football with the pig's inflated bladder.

One winter, severe frost turned the roadside pond into a playground, and the young people were soon enjoying themselves. Several long slides the full length of the pond were soon made with hob-nailed boots. We could slide only in the evenings, but in bright moonlight it seemed as light as day; the candles in jamjars were quite unnecessary. Responding to the cry, 'Keep the pot boiling', we were soon aglow with exhilaration.

It all came to an end one evening when a young man and his sister brought their skates. They were soon flying gracefully to and fro and cutting our slides to shreds. The speed of their movements and their gyrations left us no room on the ice. Grumbling and disappointed, we departed, leaving the skaters the freedom of our pond, and the moonlight.

To Banbury Cross

A delightful summer break enjoyed by the whole family was the annual day out to Banbury, usually in August, to sell the wool. Between fifteen and twenty fleeces were rammed tightly into sacks which were then wedged under the seat and behind it, with the tailboard at an angle of about 45 degrees. Dad and Mother, with my 3-year-old brother between them, filled up the front seat, while my sister and I sat on the sacks behind them – a comfortable ride for the thirteen-mile journey.

Banbury, a busy, bustling market town, was thronged with people a-foot, horse-drawn vehicles and livestock on market day, and all in such a hurry that it seemed difficult to move without being roughly jostled. Especially busy was the inn yard where the wool was weighed, graded and paid for. When the trap was empty, Kitty was unhitched and put in a stable behind the inn.

Carriers' carts, most of them covered vans with their owners' names painted on the sides in big, bold letters, were everywhere. Inn yards and streets were full of them. From most the horses had been taken out, and the carts, vans and traps stood with their shafts turned up out of the way, their tips pointing skywards like the mast of a fleet of yachts in harbour.

Besides the busy market stalls, including a sweet stall at which we stared goggle-eyed, we also saw cattle being held for sale in the street. Some were tethered, others were being held in groups by the sellers waiting for buyers to come along. Banbury livestock auction mart was opened a few years later, in 1925. It prospered and grew and now claims to be 'the Stockyard of Europe'.

There were no soft bags of wool to sit on when we loaded up to return home, so the rear seat was put in position behind the driving-seat, whose back-rest served both front and rear passengers. The ride, facing backwards, was much less comfortable than on the outward journey, but once Kitty's head was turned facing homewards, she needed no flick of the reins on her rump to spur her into a high-speed trot. We were tired, but in the basket under the seat was a large packet of 'Banbury rock', and there were some Banbury cakes for tea.

The old cottage in the fields, though unoccupied, was neither deserted nor neglected. A few bits of furniture left behind in 1916, including a grandfather clock that didn't 'go' and curtains still hanging at the windows, gave the place something of a lived-in appearance. If Dad had been trying to convince himself that nothing had changed, even though the family had moved out, the cats asleep in the sun and the hens taking vigorous dustbaths in the rickyard helped to foster the illusion. Great care was taken to see that the house was kept in reasonable repair, in case it might be needed by a member of the family sometime in the future, though such a possibility seemed remote indeed. Dad had a deep affection for the old place and sometimes said it meant more to him than did the large, imposing house in the village, though how anyone could be so sentimental about such a 'dump' I didn't understand.

The empty cottage came to life during haymaking, when door and windows were thrown open, admitting fresh air and sunshine, though we children preferred to play outdoors, where we had tremendous fun romping in the hot, prickly hay.

For me, the oldest, playing days seemed to come to an end all too soon. At about nine or ten I was considered capable of using a fork for certain jobs, such as helping to pass hay across the rick to the 'rick-builder', but my first assignment was to lead the horse pulling the wagon, guiding it between the rows of hay while two men pitched huge forkfuls of hay to the one building the load. When the hay was very dry and light, and the ground hard and uneven, building a load of loose hay which would stay on the wagon until the rickyard was reached was almost impossible, so it was securely bound on with a rope, but even that was no guarantee against mishap, though a 'shed' load was a very rare occurrence.

My town-bred uncles always enjoyed lending a hand with the hay whenever they were visiting, but not one of them ever acquired the knack of using a hayfork. In their hands the simple two-pronged tool became a deadly weapon. They would get a little hay on the fork and lift it up waist-high, as though they were carrying it on a shovel, the prongs pointing menacingly forward, but before they had carried it a yard, the hay would fall to the ground. A lot of sweat and a lot of puffing and grunting, but very little to show for their efforts, yet Dad was always pleased to see them, glad of all the help he could get – skilled and unskilled. With a strong gang in the field, work would sometimes continue until eleven o'clock or later in the evening but still not completely dark at that time of year. At a distance you might not have been able to make out the workers or guess what they were doing but an occasional snatch of conversation – 'Where d'ye want it, Jack?' and the reply, 'Front corner' – would have told you exactly what was happening; and you would have heard quite distinctly the creak of the wagon each time it moved forward a few paces. In settled weather the last load might be left standing in the field overnight.

However late we stayed in the field, there were still the chores to be done when we eventually reached home, and it was sometimes past midnight before we had milked the cows, separated the milk and fed the calves. Fortunately haymaking could advance quite quickly in a spell of hot weather. Crops were usually light, and cutting seldom began before the middle of July, by which time most of the grasses were dead ripe. Such crops as these were half-made hay before they were cut and needed little drying in the field before they were ready to stack. Years later, scientists informed us that our easily made hay was not very nutritious.

The lush, heavily fertilized grass now cut in June would

have been too much for men and women with forks and rakes, and for horse-drawn machinery to handle. A man on a tractor, belting round a field with a power-driven, high-speed machine can cope with the heaviest crop, though it be literally oozing with sap. Even so, dry weather and sunshine are still needed to make good hay and, these essentials to good haymaking being at a premium in Britain, farmers now ensure high-quality winter feed for their stock by converting all that lush grass into silage. But there is a snag. The black liquid which oozes from the stack is highly toxic, and farmers can be heavily fined for allowing it to escape into a water-course. Some farmers maintain that a cow's digestive system is better suited to dealing with hay.

Mother, a regular church-goer before her marriage, had been unable to attend during her years at the remote cottage, but she began again soon after her return to the village. Though the church was a mile from home, she often took me with her, leaving Dad in charge of the two younger children. The first time I sat in the hushed silence of that lofty, ill-lit building wondering what was going to happen, I'm sure I would have been very frightened without Mother's reassuring presence. Then music suddenly broke into the silence, though where it was coming from I couldn't make out. At that time I didn't know that a little old lady was working away behind the red curtain near the pulpit.

We all stood up when boys and men in white robes began walking up the church, followed by a tall, bald-headed man also in white but with a long, bright red thing hanging down his back. I admired – indeed, I believe I coveted – that gorgeous piece of silk the moment I set eyes on it, and wondered whether one day I might have one like it. In my innocence I had no idea that between me and that piece of red silk stretched an unbridgable gulf. The building, the music, the singing and reading combined to create an atmosphere which, though it over-awed me somewhat at first, I grew to love.

When my brother and sister were old enough to attend church, Mother took them along, and Dad, no longer able to offer a reasonable excuse for staying behind, tagged along. To everyone's surprise, he took to it like a duck to water. As present tenant of the glebe originally let to his father, Dad had been acquainted with the vicar for some years; now, meeting on a different footing, they quickly became friends. Dad was soon serving as sidesman, was then confirmed and shortly afterwards was elected to the office of churchwarden. As landlord and tenant, Parson John and Dad understood each other perfectly; as vicar and churchwarden they got along like a house on fire.

Farming prospered throughout the war years and for a few years afterwards, and optimistic farmers were buying farms left, right and centre. Dad sold a freshly calved Shorthorn cow for the unbelievable price of £55, and two stall-fed bullocks for over £40 each, while corn, hay and straw were indeed a 'seller's market'. In fact, things were going so well with us that in 1921 my parents decided that they could afford to send me to the grammar school in Leamington Spa. It was a day school, and the fees, if I remember correctly, were 3 guineas a term. I, and a cousin who started at the same time, lodged with an aunt and uncle who lived in the town within easy walking-distance of the school. The aunt was Dad's oldest sister, Mary, who, though I didn't know it at the time, had so diligently kept a diary when she was a girl back in the last century. Now a comfortably built, middle-aged matron, she was still deeply interested in the written word. In her home were many books, all of a high moral tone, but she did not ask us to read them; instead, she read aloud to us, a chapter or two each evening from an edifying book of her choice.

In no time at all she was coaxing, persuading and prompting me, the older of her two nephews, to write a poem and submit it to the school magazine. We set to work together, and at the end of term a short poem entitled 'Football' appeared in the magazine above my name. Auntie, was, of course, tickled pink; I was much less excited, knowing how little I had contributed to its composition.

Two years later I was again writing a poem for possible publication in the magazine, and again I had no option. Our form master strode into the classroom one morning after assembly with a very pained expression on his face, and we guessed that we were the cause of his distress. He quickly enlightened us. He said he was downright ashamed to learn that not a single contribution for the magazine had been received from his form, but as it was not yet too late to put matters right: our lesson for that 'period' would be to write a short poem on 'Autumn'. Of the twenty or so exercises handed in at the end of the lesson, mine was selected for publication. This time I did walk an inch or two taller.

A number of boys and girls from villages in the area were obtaining scholarships to grammar school but found it almost impossible to get to town. After persistent agitation by parents, backed up by their parish councils, some convenient trains were laid on, including one to our nearest station, three miles from the village. Very few villages were lucky enough to be near a station.

I quickly made known to my parents my dislike of town life and that I hankered for home and the fields. I especially liked being at home with the family at haymaking time. On the last day of term one year, Mother drove the pony and trap into Leamington to do some shopping and to collect me, and when I asked her whether haymaking had started and she replied that it had, I was quite disappointed, and so, after some pleading on my part, I was allowed to travel from home each day by train.

The three-mile cycle ride to the station was pleasant enough in fine weather, but one very wet morning I arrived there soaked to the skin. The engine-driver noticed my bedraggled condition and, calling me to him, he and his fireman hauled me up onto the footplate, where I stood in front of the roaring fire while the fireman stoked the fire with coal. The half-hour journey did not give the fire, hot though it was, sufficient time to dry out my clothes, and the knees of my long trousers were sending out clouds of steam when we pulled into Leamington station.

That ride on the engine was a great adventure and gave me something to talk about for weeks, although my travelling schoolmates weren't too pleased with me, nor did I realize that it might have cost the engine-driver his job.

Of Christmas 1922 I have only the vaguest recollection. For once, I don't believe I groped around on Christmas morning hoping to find a book or two on the table beside my bed. In fact, I had a high temperature and was in for a nasty attack of pneumonia. I remember the doctor's telling Mother to slap hot poultices on me and as soon as one cooled to apply another. The 'crisis' came and went, though I knew nothing of it, but I suppose my parents were relieved to see me still in the land of the living.

One Sunday afternoon I was sitting by the fire with a blanket round my knees when Mother showed a visitor into the room. If I hadn't been so weak, I believe I would have jumped clean out of my skin when I saw who it was – the headmaster of the grammar school. He came across the room and sat in a chair facing me on the opposite side of the hearth. I was quite taken aback at first and for a few minutes was somewhat over-awed by the presence of the great man. I was accustomed to rising at his entrance into the big hall at school and standing while he strode up the centre aisle to the rostrum to lead prayers, his gown billowing out as he went. Now he seemed quite human, and he quickly succeeded in setting me at ease.

Arnold Thornton was a local preacher, and he explained that he had come over from Leamington to take evening service at the Congregational chapel in the village and was having tea with some neighbours of ours who were Congregationalists. That he should know of my existence, and of my illness, and that he was prepared to go out of his way to visit me on a Sunday afternoon, was difficult to believe. That he did know all about me, that I was more than one among a sea of faces in the assembly hall or simply a number on his register, was reassuring, young as I was. I'm sure his visit did me more good than a dozen bottles of the doctor's bitter-tasting medicine.

After twenty odd years in the parish Parson John retired, and he and his wife moved to Leamington. He was a passenger on the school train one morning and walked into town ahead of me and my companions. When he stopped and waited for us to catch up with him, we began to wonder what we had done wrong. However, it was me he wanted, and taking me on one side he said he had a most important errand for me. He said he had stayed behind to make a few last-minute calls after his wife had moved out with the furniture the previous afternoon, and that he had spent the night in the empty vicarage. He went on to say that he had left in a hurry that morning to catch the early train and that to his dismay he now found he still had the keys with him. He then gave me two large bunches of keys, charging me to take great care of them and hand them over to my father the moment I got home in the evening. It was probably the first time those keys had been out of his safekeeping since the day he moved to the parish.

The keys were those of the vicarage and the church. They made quite a heavy bundle but I decided to keep them with me through the day, and though I was a little puffed up by the tremendous importance of the errand, I was also glad to get home with them and be relieved of their weight and the responsibility. Those were the first church keys entrusted to my care.

Our nearest neighbours, whose large farmhouse stood only fifty yards from ours across a small paddock, were a middle-aged couple with a growing family who had taken over the farm shortly after the end of the war.

With one daughter, a girl of about my own age, I became great friends. I, at the grand old age of eleven, thought Myra was rather special. One of her evening chores was to take her turn at shutting up the hens for the night and collecting the eggs. I knew roughly the time she would be setting out for one particular fowl-house, three fields from home, and whenever I could wangle it, I accompanied her on her errand across the fields. On several pleasant summer evenings we sat on the grass and waited for the last lingering forager to disappear through the pop-hole. Once Myra was collecting eggs from the nest-boxes when she called me in to take the eggs from under a squawking broody hen protecting her nest by darting out her sharp beak at any attempt to put a hand near her. No knight in shining armour ever felt more chivalrous than I did. Though I longed for more opportunities to display my valour, none occurred.

At this distance in time I remember little else of those enjoyable evening walks except that our way led through a field of mowing grass, a thin, bendy crop sprinkled with buttercups and wide-eyed moon daisies.

As soon as the war was over, farmers began putting arable land down to grass, and when financial help from the Corn Production Act came to an end, the return to pasture became a stampede. This time Dad went with it and grassed down the whole of his eight-acre arable field, including the two-acre plot that had been in cultivation without a break since it had first been broken in the 1890s. No expensive grass seeds were purchased; instead, seeds were collected from the cows' mangers during the winter and broadcast on the field in the spring, weed seeds and dust included. Dad was a great believer in the value of basic-slag, a by-product of the once busy steel industry and a valuable phosphatic fertilizer, and gave the field a good dressing. The result was amazing. Clover plants quickly covered bare patches of ground, and two or three years later came a good year for clover. The whole field was covered with a snow-white carpet so deliciously scented that you could almost drink the heady fragrance from half a mile away.

The return to grass signalled the return to depression, and in 1924 my parents realized that they could no longer afford to keep me on at grammar school. The headmaster wrote to them, pointing out the advantages of keeping me at school until I was at least sixteen, but it was of no avail, and at the end of the term in which I reached my fourteenth birthday my schooldays came to an abrupt end. It was no consolation to me to know that the headmaster had thought sufficiently well of me and my work to want me to continue at his school.

My parents knew only too well that they would never be able to do for my brother and sister what they had done for me – farming had again slumped disastrously, and farm prices were back to pre-war levels. The boy who helped Dad on the farm was paid off but went straight to a better-paid job at the brickworks. A growing boy is a hungry boy, which was probably why nothing was said to me about wages; even the occasional bit of pocket-money was hard to come by.

In 1920 Dad had received the alarming news that our house was up for sale. The price being asked was £1,500, and as sitting tenant he was offered first refusal. The price was way out of his reach, and the offer was declined. A few people came and nosed around but, with a sitting tenant who intended to remain sitting unless well compensated, the sale eventually fell through. Six years later the house was on the market again, and this time it was bought for £750. By 1926 the war-time boom in farming was already history, and many farmers who had borrowed heavily and optimistically to buy their farms suddenly found themselves in serious trouble. Dad counted himself a lucky man – his neighbours had tried to persuade him to buy, the first time round. He was lucky that he couldn't afford it, and that Mother would have none of it.

In 1924 we were still making butter and selling it to the carrier, but some farmers had discovered an easier and much more profitable way of making a living. From towns and cities all over the country was coming an ever-increasing demand for milk. A farmer near Rugby was advertising fresh milk, delivered in the town, at 9 pence a quart, and added, 'A postcard will ensure the cart calling the following morning.' The townsman's appetite for milk appeared insatiable.

Advertisements from dairies in Coventry, Birmingham and London asked for milk to be put on rail at the farmer's nearest station. Some dairies offered to settle accounts weekly. Wilts United Dairies appeared on the scene about this time, and they picked up milk at the farm gate with a motor lorry. Dairies pointed out in their persuasive advertisements that milk-selling, was easier than butter-making. Dad, like most of his neighbours, could not resist the temptation. Milk-selling was so easy. You simply milked the cows, ran the milk over a cooler and stood it at the gate in churns supplied by the dairy. No twice-daily separating, no churning, no messy butter-making. Farmers' wives saw an end to drudgery in the dairy. Life would never be the same again. It all sounded too good to be true and, indeed, it proved to be so before many months had passed.

Farmers sold their milk under contracts drawn up by the

purchaser, and they soon discovered whose interests were favoured in the documents they had been so eager to sign. There were penalties (deductions) for sending more or less than the quantity stated in the contract, although some fluctuation was allowed within a narrow band. Producers were frequently being notified that a day's consignment was short of the quantity stated on the ticket accompanying the milk, and what were considered excessive charges for collection were a constant cause of disagreement. It was a very unsatisfactory state of affairs, and repeated attempts to secure just contracts, fair prices and reasonable collection charges failed to improve matters; instead, they gave rise to considerable bitterness between producer and purchaser.

Dad returned one day, very distressed, from a meeting in Banbury between a gathering of angry farmers and a hard-line, unsympathetic representative of the dairy. It had been an unpleasant confrontation, but the dairy's arrogant 'take it or leave it' attitude was more than many producers could swallow, and a number, including Dad, returned to butter-making. Their wives were far from pleased at the decision their husbands had taken. Men, they said, had no idea how much work was involved in butter-making. Meanwhile, the dairies were confident that, like the spider, they had only to sit back and wait; nor did they have long to wait before farmers were drifting back, cap in hand, prepared to sign on the dotted line, and on terms no better than before.

A few years later the Milk Marketing Board came into being, and this was, without doubt, the salvation of many small producers during the thirties. Dairy herds were small, the average being somewhere between six and twelve milkers, or about what one man was prepared to milk by hand but on which his livelihood depended.

The board brought order and stability to a chaotic but rapidly expanding industry – an industry with many small producers for whom the monthly milk cheque was their lifeline. The smallest producer no longer felt himself to be at the mercy of some faceless purchaser. However, the stability and better prospects brought about by the Milk Marketing Board encouraged the progressive farmer to increase the size of his herd and to invest in a milking-machine – the first steps in the revolution of the dairy industry which progressed steadily over the next forty years.

In the spring of 1924 a 'mission' took place in the village, though for once it was not the Methodists but the staid old Church of England which set out to rouse the spiritual life of the parish.

The missioners were two young Church Army men who travelled from village to village in a horse-drawn caravan, though they possessed no horse. At the end of their stay in a parish a farmer volunteered, with a nudge from the vicar perhaps, to haul the text-covered caravan to the next village, where the horses would be unhitched and brought home. From there another volunteer would take the 'mission' a stage further on its journey.

During their stay the missioners were able to contact almost every man, woman and child in the parish. A chat by a cottage fireside, over a garden gate or on the village green was an approach very different from that made nowadays by the high-powered, expensively promoted evangelist who is able to stir mass emotions at large, central venues, but the personal 'one to one' method is probably as effective and as enduring.

The services held in church were informal, bright and lively, and the children were taught a number of catchy choruses, some of which were sung in Sunday School for years afterwards.

The mission concluded with a 'magic lantern' service in church. Extra help was needed to take the collection, so Dad thrust a bag in my hand. Almost the only light came from the lantern which beamed on the screen stretched across the chancel arch and, while we collected in semi-darkness, the hymn 'Just as I am, without one plea' was sung. The refrain, 'O Lamb of God, I come', rang in my head for days.

Probably because village life was so uneventful, with little going on to enliven evenings or weekends, I found that service both exciting and moving, though whether it was a 'religious experience', as is generally understood by that term, is very doubtful.

6

To be a farmer's boy

In December 1924 I left school to begin life as a farmer's boy, and I was far from thrilled at the prospect. No field work was in progress but there was work to be done and a daily routine to follow. Dad set off after breakfast every morning to fodder the cattle in the fields while I was left behind to muck out the cowsheds, feed the calves and saw and chop wood for the fire.

After only a few weeks I became bored, and in the afternoons when time dragged heavily I climbed the wall-ladder to the hay-loft, where I had hidden away among the cobwebs a pencil, a rib-handled school pen with a 'J' nib, a bottle of Stephens ink and a notebook. There, seated on a truss of hay in front of a small window with no glass in it, I tried writing descriptive paragraphs about the countryside, like those then appearing in the *Daily Mail* above the initials P.W.D.I. (Percy Izzard). I liked some of them so much that I tried to learn them by heart.

One afternoon, while I tried to write in that freezing-cold loft, snowflakes drifted in through the window and, falling on my paper, melted as they fell. I remember trying to describe the eerie silence in the farmyard following a heavy fall of snow the previous night. The only sounds to be heard were the grunting of the pig in his sty, asking for his evening meal, and the fluttering wings of a dozen sparrows desperately seeking shelter for the night 'beneath the snow-hung eaves of the cowshed', as I so brilliantly described the scene.

On winter evenings there was little to do but read, and

when I grew tired of that, I tried writing articles and short stories which with youthful optimism I dispatched to busy London editors. I should have known better.

One winter, while I was busy writing the opening chapters of what was to be a gripping adventure yarn – on the lines of a 'Dick Turpin'-type book I had recently been reading – my brother and a school friend used their free time to some purpose. A Saturday 'meet' of foxhounds sometimes kept them busy most of the day. Dashing across fields, they opened gates and then rummaged around in the mud for pennies thrown down by riders as they splashed through the miry gateways.

A second enterprise of theirs was mole-catching. They set traps around the fields and proved themselves quite successful trappers; nor did they flinch at the unsavoury task of skinning the creatures and part-curing the skins. They found a market for them through an advertisement in the farming press, and received a much better price than they would from the wandering gypsies who called all too frequently for rags, bones and rabbit skins. I have no idea how much they were paid for the skins, but I do recall numerous attempts to estimate how many soft little moles' jackets would be required to make one full-length fur coat.

However, their initiative and enterprise brought them useful pocket-money while my scribbling in an old exercise book showed no profit. Theirs was a bird in the hand, mine still in the bush – and likely to remain there.

A week or two before Christmas the yard resounded to the most frightful, ear-splitting scream, a sound as much a part of country life and as pleasing to the ear to many people as the song of the nightingale – it had been decided to 'have the pig down', and the pig was objecting. Previously I had been at school or had managed to disappear when the butcher arrived, but now the moment had come when I was needed to take an active part in the proceedings, and though I was scared stiff at the prospect, I knew I had to stay and see it through. I would have been even more scared to run away – I could never have looked my father in the face again. When I was handed the heart and lights, dripping with blood, and told to 'hang it up somewhere', I gripped it firmly and took it and hung it on a nail near the kitchen door, and no one appeared to notice that I had been almost paralysed with terror while carrying out that simple task.

After it was all over, I carefully scraped up every last scrap of fire-blackened, blood-stained straw, and with the yard broom and several buckets of water I did my best to clean off every trace of the blood already drying on wall and floor where the pig had bled to death, but I was not entirely successful. However, later in the day we all enjoyed a meal of pig's fry (odd scraps of this and that), including some delicious liver with a few onions added, and there were still mouth-watering bone and pork pies to look forward to – Mother's pies were always special.

On a later occasion the pig-killer turned up at the appointed time but Dad was nowhere to be found. The butcher slipped on his apron and sharpened a knife on the 'steel' hanging from his waist until, when he tested it on his forearm, it whisked off the hairs as sweetly as a razor would. He was a busy man, and after waiting only a few minutes for Dad to put in an appearance he said, 'We'll have to manage on our own, Ray.' My heart sank as he turned and headed for the pig-sty and its doomed inmate. He entered the sty and a moment later had succeeded in slipping a blood-stained cord under its jaw. When it began to scream, he shouted, 'Grab his tail!' Thus do 'persons of a nervous disposition' come to terms with reality. The pig had fulfilled its destiny – that was how we came to have bacon in the house to feed us through the winter.

During my first winter as farm boy we were making butter, and I soon discovered what was entailed. On a cold morning, although I usually stood on a thick sack, my feet soon became blocks of ice as I turned the handle of the large butter churn. The cream would sometimes flop around the inside of the churn for ages, and then, when I expected the butter to arrive, everything would go very quiet and the handle would spin round at a touch as though it were quite empty. The cream had, in fact frothed up and stuck around the inside of the churn, as light as the lightest whipped cream. It had, as we said, 'gone to sleep'. Mother would very occasionally pour a little warm water into the churn to release the cream and speed up the arrival of the butter, but she did it reluctantly – it was the lazy dairymaid's remedy, she said, though once in a while, in very cold weather, it was necessary. A few minutes later I would hear the heavy plop of butter in the churn.

My task done, Mother's was about to begin. After washing, salting and making up the butter into pats, the equipment had to be thoroughly cleaned before it could be put away. The only materials used for the cleaning were lots of scalding-hot water, a scrubbing-brush, sometimes a little washing soda and always plenty of elbow grease, but when she had finished scalding and scrubbing, no bug stood a chance of getting a foothold in her dairy.

The return to pasture following the post-war collapse in corn prices meant a return to livestock farming, and that was, as it had always been, a very risky business. At that time vets were unable to offer much help when animals fell sick, and losses were sometimes heavy. Sheep were vulnerable to a number of diseases now easily controlled by simple, routine treatment. Flocks could be decimated by liver fluke, kidney disease or lung and stomach worms. One year a farmer near us went out every morning with a horse and cart to pick up dead animals struck down by a pestilence, probably worms, from which only a few survived. Cattle succumbed to tuberculosis, johnnes disease and worms, while contagious abortion was a scourge all cattle-breeders feared, and there is no doubt that some animals died from malnutrition – starvation due to the lack of the right kind of food during the winter months.

Many pastures became dense jungles of spear and creeping thistles during late summer – jungles into which the boldest dog would be reluctant to enter in search of the odd sheep that had found a small clearing in which it could lie and hope to escape the tormenting flies; a sick, maggot-infested animal would suffer a slow, painful death unless the flock was counted and inspected daily. In hot 'maggoty' weather, good shepherds on our small lowland farms checked their flocks early in the morning and again in the cool of the evening.

Many pastures, especially those at a distance from the

farmstead, were covered with ant-hills, some of them as big as an upturned wheelbarrow and so thick on the ground that they almost touched each other. It was impossible to operate a machine of any kind in fields in such a terrible condition, with the result that they became even more neglected, and even less profitable. Attempts were made to cut the thistles with scythes when work was slack at the back end of summer, but it was then too late to prevent underground roots storing up energy, and seeds being blown far and wide – too late to prevent a still heavier crop of weeds the following year. It was a sorry state of affairs, and farmers were naturally very bitter and felt badly let down when they realized that they were needed only in time of war. Things were so bad that some landlords agreed to lower rents; others, more cautious, grudgingly allowed rebates.

About this time Dad decided to plough up his original two-acre plot once again. Buying every scrap of straw needed for thatching and bedding, and buying in every ounce of stock feed, did not make sense now that he had a hungry young man to keep fully occupied. However, making the decision to plough was one thing, carrying out the work another. It would have been too much for our two horses, but a part-time local farmer with a team of heavy horses to feed jumped at the chance of earning a little extra money. 'My horses never stop eating,' he said. 'They keep twisting hay down 'em without stopping to chew the cud.'

George, probably in his late fifties, weather-beaten and slightly round-shouldered, loved horses and enjoyed nothing better than working with them. He was a born ploughman, and it was a treat to watch him at work. While the horses had a 'blow', as he called it, at the end of the furrow, he would take a short-stemmed black pipe from his pocket and light up, but he took good care not to pause long enough to allow the horses to become cold or stiff, and after only a couple of minutes he would slip the still-smoking pipe into his waistcoat pocket and take up the lines. As the chains tightened and the horses began to feel the dead pull of the plough behind them, he would shout, 'Gee-up, Blossom! You've got it again,' and the plough, moving slowly forward, would begin turning another furrow, leaving behind it the lingering aroma of George's tobacco mingled with the smell of freshly turned earth and autumn leaves. Overhead, rooks cawed and wheeled to the musical accompaniment of jingling harness and the occasional squeak of a plough wheel.

A few days after the work had been completed I saw Dad carefully studying the plot, and after he had completed his visual survey, he said he didn't think it was quite two acres. He then paced it and, after making some mental calculations, pronounced that a strip roughly ten yards wide running the full length of the plot was needed to make the magical two acres. A few days later he produced two forks and was soon instructing me in the art of using a two-tined fork for breaking up turf. I found it extremely heavy work. Though I was probably wrong, I suspected him of having deliberately engineered an opportunity of demonstrating in a very practical way just how hard had been the task he and his father had undertaken in that grim first year at the farm.

When Parson John left the parish, the churchwardens were faced with the responsibility of finding clergy to conduct Sunday services during the interregnum, and spare clergy were hard to come by. The rural dean, who always has special responsibilities at these times, gave Dad the addresses of two retired parsons in Leamington who, he thought, might prove helpful. Dad gave me those two addresses and sent me off on my push-bike to 'interview' these two possible 'temps'. I was still in my fourteenth year, nearly sixty-five years ago, since when I have known and have had dealings with more parsons than I have had hot dinners.

I called first on Mr Simmonds, a short, lightly built man with a small pointed beard and a sharp, brusque manner of speech – a prickly little character, he seemed to me. He soon made it plain that, with transport being so difficult and help needed every week, he could not undertake such a responsibility.

My second call was on a Mr Waters, white-haired and rather frail but with a warm, friendly manner which made him easy to talk to. Like Mr Simmonds, he said he could not undertake duties on a weekly basis, although he did say he was sorry he couldn't help us. With youthful effrontery, I then suggested that perhaps he and Mr Simmonds might get together and come to some arrangement between them for sharing the duties. This they must have done, since between them they took the Sunday services for several months, until the older and frailer of the two was knocked down and killed by a motor car while crossing the road near his home, when, of course, the other man withdrew his services.

The rural dean then came along with a man who, he assured the churchwardens, would fill the breach perfectly until a new vicar was appointed. The man was a bachelor, fit and extremely energetic; his name I cannot recall. He said that if he could sleep at the vicarage and have the use of the kitchen he would be on hand in case of any emergency; he could also take weekday services, visit the sick and make himself generally useful in the parish; and so permission was given for him to move into the vicarage. He very quickly showed himself to be a truly conscientious pastor. He was also interested in church music and proceeded to sharpen up the choir and widen their repertoire of hymns.

Everything went swimmingly until a new vicar was appointed. The Revd X was terribly upset when he heard the news. He wanted to know why he was being turned out and asked whether he hadn't been doing a satisfactory job. He said he intended to stay, and when the new vicar's wife turned up to measure the windows for new curtains, he was far from polite to her. He dug in his heels and refused to move.

When the authorities could see that he really intended being awkward, they took action. The archdeacon, a diocesan legal boffin, the rural dean and two churchwardens descended on him in a body, prepared to inform him that, unless he left within a certain time, he would be evicted. There was no scene, no fuss; the good man had merely 'tried it on' and was ready to surrender. Without a disagreeable word being spoken he undertook to leave without further delay. Shortly afterward he folded his tent and quietly stole away – his destination unknown. Whether he had friends or relations no one knew.

We all felt extremely sorry for him, but 'rules is rules'. The mistake was in allowing him into the vicarage in the first place. I am reminded of him each time I hear the hymn 'Sun of My Soul', sung to 'Abends', one of the tunes he taught us.

I launched my first farming enterprise in 1925. Mother loaned me a broody hen and supplied me with a 'sitting' of thirteen eggs of the popular Rhode Island Red breed to put under her. I made a nest for her in a corner of one of the bedrooms in the empty cottage, not realizing that the site I had selected was most unsuitable for the purpose. The dry wooded floor and the warmth of the hen's body·could have led to serious loss of moisture from the eggs (dehydration, they call it these days) and the complete failure of my enterprise, but Mother must have known a thing or two about the incubation of eggs when she advised me to sprinkle them liberally with water daily for the last ten days of incubation. The hatch turned out quite well, though I do not remember the exact number of chicks the old hen brought off. I know I was very proud of them, and watching the bright-eyed little creatures trying to pick up the food I had put down for them gave me pleasure and satisfaction.

Somebody had told me that Anconas (a small black-and-white breed) were marvellous layers, so in 1926 I decided to try a sitting. Six months later I was to discover that, though the active little birds turned out a good number of large, white eggs, they were extremely nervous and shy. They preferred to roost in a tree rather than in the fowl-house, and they laid their eggs in all kinds of odd places; they would make a nest in a clump of nettles, in the middle of a thick hedge or in some inaccessible place in one of the outbuildings – anywhere except in the nest-boxes provided for them.

Though it was late in the season, about the middle of May, I put a broody hen on a nest and settled her down in readiness for the eggs I had arranged to collect from a smallholder who also kept a public house on the far side of the village.

Despite the fact that Myra, now in her teens, was away in domestic service, we still managed to meet from time to time, and being at home when my eggs were ready for collection, she accompanied me one evening. We left the road and followed a well-trodden footpath leading through a meadow where red and roan cattle grazed, over a stile, across a cornfield and alongside a crop of beans in full flower, filling the air with a most delicious scent – a pleasant, leisurely walk of about a mile. Around midsummer we were able to enjoy the same walk again when I was sent to collect a church bell-rope from the Coventry carrier. It was a perfect summer evening, and on our return we lingered for a while at a stile from which we had a splendid view over miles of beautiful Warwickshire countryside. The meadow was golden with buttercups, poppies edged the footpath through the corn, and dog-roses of many shades of pink hung on the hedges.

Myra sat on the stile while I stood near her with my back to it, and once, when she bent down to speak to me, a tress of her hair, probably not more than one or two strands, moved by the lightest of evening breezes, very, very softly caressed my cheek, though I doubt whether she was aware of it. Such odd trivialities does memory lock away. A few months later the family left the village, and Myra and I lost touch.

From poultry-keeping I graduated into the pig-fattening business, beginning with the purchase of a single pig. A farmer with a litter of newly weaned, 8-week-old youngsters for sale told me he was charging 35 shillings apiece for them, but as I was only a young chap just making a start, I could have one for 32s.6d. The moment he entered the sty, the little pigs began dashing madly round him, darting between his legs and slipping through his hands, but he eventually succeeded in seizing one, apparently at random, which he deftly dropped into the sack I was holding in readiness. I handed over my precious money and set off for home, less than 200 yards away, my pig struggling and grunting in the sack slung over my shoulder. Much to my disappointment, it looked considerably smaller in its new home than it had in the farmer's sty, nor had I noticed at the time that its head was almost as big as its body.

My father's comments on my business acumen were not very encouraging either. 'You've been done, Raymond,' he said, and went on without tact or sympathy, 'Old John saw you coming. He's palmed the dillin' off on you – but you'll learn.' It was a painful first lesson in stock-buying, but it did not make the farmer a villain, for all that, simply a good salesman, while I had been the victim of my own enthusiasm and inexperience.

I was fortunate enough to find a local buyer for my pig

when the time came to turn it into cash, and it was the first of a number I sold to the same young man over a period of several years. He worked on an adjoining farm, though originally trained as a butcher, and augmented his farm wage by killing a lamb or a pig from time to time and selling it round the village, having previously collected orders for the meat.

The sale of a pig followed a set pattern. To begin with, we agreed that the price per score should be that published in the local paper of average returns at the auction marts for that particular week. We then had to agree on the weight of the pig as it stood in the sty, but that never proved difficult and very little haggling took place. My pigs averaged between three and four score each in weight, took around nine weeks to fatten and at a pound a score brought in £3 – £4. Net profit over food costs was about £1 on each transaction, which I considered a fair reward for my labour.

Soon after his arrival the new vicar made it known that he hoped to do a bit of fox-hunting. He had no hunter of his own, nor did he buy one, and if he expected a local farmer to provide one for him, he was disappointed. His hunting plans came to nothing.

He prepared me and four other young people for confirmation. We were admitted at the back door of the vicarage, where we sat on benches in the kitchen while blackbirds sang to us from the garden.

The vicar's wife attended church but never stayed to speak to any of the congregation after the service, and she was rarely seen in the village. It seemed as though she had taken an instant dislike to the place and had already decided she would have no part of it.

Both the vicar and his wife were obviously disappointed with what they found in their new parish. The vicar was a pleasant, likeable fellow and would probably have succeeded in adapting himself to the life had he had a different partner. As it was, their stay with us was a short one, a little over two years.

7

Ding, dong, merrily on high

The first field work to be undertaken every spring was the harrowing and rolling of the pastures to pull out old dead grass and to level ground churned up by cattle during the winter. The jingling of the chain harrows travelling backwards and forwards across the field leaving alternate strips of dark and light green was a tonic – it gave an uplift to the spirits, as though bells were announcing the arrival of spring.

However, we had no chain-harrows: we used muck-forks to scatter cowpats and molehills – 'clatting', the old folks called it. But we did have a roller made from a tree-trunk. It was about twelve inches in diameter and eight feet wide. Sitting on the frame of the roller while the horse plodded slowly backwards and forwards across the field was one of the easier and more enjoyable jobs I had to do. The horse would not be hurried and maintained his steady pace from start to finish. Without an engine roaring in our ears, we could hear as well as see the distressed nesting peewits diving and tumbling around us, and we could hear, though we might not see, the larks high overhead rejoicing in the spring sunshine.

Much of our haymaking was still done by hand and involved the whole family, although we did have a few ancient implements, probably purchased second-hand in Grandfather's time. The only modern machine we possessed was a two-horse grass-mower which I was not allowed to take out until I was older. Handling a pair of horses and a mowing-machine requires strength and skill.

My first attempt at mowing was made with a 'Walter A. Wood', one-horse machine, though I wouldn't have said it was the ideal beginner's tool. If the horse did not walk fast enough to maintain the knife at cutting-speed or if the knife were blunt, the mower would stall, the wheels would rise two feet into the air, and the rider, unless he clung tightly to the seat, ran the risk of being thrown in front of the cutter-bar.

Our horse-rake was a primitive contraption and lacked that most important component – a seat. Theoretically, the operator walked behind the rake, guiding the horse with the reins in one hand and at the same time doing his best to tip and empty the rake with the other hand as he walked along, but someone with the strength and agility of a superman would have been needed to perform the feat, and so two people usually went with the man-killing old relic.

One very hot day, with the sun burning down out of a steely-blue sky, we had a few acres of well-made hay ready to be raked into rows and carted. Unfortunately Dad was suffering with a touch of gastric trouble, so Mother went with me to the hayfield. We poured oil on a number of likely places on the rake and backed the horse between the shafts. The intense heat shimmered and danced over the sun-baked hay as we set off across the field. I led the horse while Mother walked behind the rake and emptied it, though not always on the intended spot, by yanking hard down on a long lever.

The heat became more oppressive as the afternoon wore on. My shirt was sticking to my back, and sweat was streaming down Mother's bright-red cheeks. We had both been much too engrossed in our task, which demanded intense concentration, to notice that the dazzling, almost blinding sun was now behind a thick haze through which it shone a dull blood-red. Threatening dark clouds began to appear, the wind freshened and a whirlwind travelling across the field spiralled hay high into the air as it went. Mother, now aware of what was brewing, decided it was time to give up, and we unhitched the horse as a jagged flash of lightning followed by a loud crack of thunder and a few large spots of rain sent us scampering for shelter.

Then the storm broke. No men came that evening to cart and stack the hay we had raked together with so much toil and sweat, and though it was eventually dried and stacked, its beautiful smell and much of its feeding-value had been lost.

Corn harvest too was still very much a family affair, though it was now a younger generation laying bonds, tying up sheaves and standing them in shooks. The day came when Dad gave me a hook and stick and set me to follow him as he hacked away with his hook and pulled the corn into sheaves. With two of us at work, he had expected great things to happen, but I was young and inexperienced and he was very disappointed with our progress. One day he threw down his hook in disgust and brought out a scythe, but the scythe was not a success either. The ripe, brittle corn stalks quickly blunted it, and he reckoned he was spending far too much time with the whetstone in his hand. Nevertheless, he was determined to get the work speeded up.

With that end in view, we dragged the old one-horse grass-mower from the back of the barn and took it to the village. Dad and the blacksmith then got their heads together and between them designed and constructed a contraption which, when fitted to the mower, would convert it into a reaping-machine. It proved reasonably successful but required two workers to go with it, one to guide the horse, the other to operate the reaping-attachment, and though it dropped the corn in bundles faintly resembling sheaves, it made extremely hard work for the rest of the family. Now, instead of laying bonds and tying up sheaves, they were kept fully occupied dragging the untied sheaves clear of the track the machine would follow on its next bout. Tying up the sheaves had to wait until cutting had finished for the day.

We usually grew about half an acre of potatoes, and one year, when we had a small surplus to dispose of, I was entrusted with the errand of delivering five or six hundredweights to a shop in Leamington. Seated on the front of the trolley, driving-reins in my hands and ten miles of open road ahead of me, I felt quite grown-up and important and thrilled to find myself on such a responsible errand, though it proved to be uneventful – no steam-rollers hissed at us, and motor cars were few and far between; nor was the load too heavy for my horse, Boxer, to haul uphill, nor too heavy for him to hold in check on downhill gradients. There was no brake on the trolley, but a heavy iron 'shoe' hung at the side for use as a brake should one be needed.

I had enough money on me for a drink and something to eat and was looking forward to getting myself a meal of some kind before setting out on the homeward journey, but when the manager of the shop pressed half a crown into my hand I was overjoyed – I could now afford to indulge myself with some of my favourite cream cakes, delicacies we rarely saw at home.

Then a fit of madness came over me, and instead of calling at a cake shop or a café I left the horse and trolley outside a large store and made for the book department in which a few years earlier I had enjoyed being let loose to select some books for a school prize. That experience had been the nearest thing to heaven on earth, certainly more exciting than walking up the large hall to collect my prize. Like most boys I enjoyed a good adventure story, and now, as then, I loitered over books by Rider-Haggard, Ballantyne and Fenimore-Cooper, but for some inexplicable reason I blew my money on a book with the exciting title *A Senior English Course*.

I expect I was very hungry when I finally arrived home. Boxer had had no food either, since setting out in the morning, but he was glad of the chance to pull over and take a long, cool drink from one of the roadside water-troughs we passed along the way, thoughtfully provided for the refreshment of thirsty horses.

What prompted the Revd Francis Aylwin and his wife to move from Tottenham, London, to our backwoods village, they never revealed, but they readily admitted that everything was very strange to them and that the new life would take a bit of getting used to.

In the early thirties they began keeping a few poultry and found the hobby so fascinating that their orchard and paddock were soon full of poultry houses, some of them quite big ones. Had you called at the vicarage, you would almost certainly have found the vicar among the poultry, and you might have recognized him by his old felt hat, open-necked khaki shirt and gumboots.

Mrs A. thoroughly enjoyed a gossip with the group who gathered round the stove after service on a winter evening, and if there was a jumble sale coming off or church decorating to do, she liked to be in the thick of it, although she was careful not to charge in and tread on tender toes. And so, gradually, the village grew on them, and they on the village.

About this time my parents got the idea that I might not be cut out for farming, and cast about in search of something more suitable for me. My sister and I had both taken music lessons, and we often played the organ at Sunday School. On the strength of this my parents decided to send me to a professional organist and teacher of music in Leamington for tuition more advanced than was available in the village. The teacher was a busy man but agreed to see me before deciding whether he could accept me as a pupil. He listened while I stumbled through half a dozen bars of a hymn he had put in front of me as a test piece, then stopped me and shook his head. A minute later I was standing on the pavement, my pride a little dented but, secretly, quite relieved.

My father then had a word with the vicar about the possibility of my being trained for the ministry. The vicar was all for it and started the ball rolling. A few weeks later the rural dean came to see me. A bustling, energetic but jovial little man, he slapped me on the back and exclaimed, 'Splendid, my lad! Splendid! I'm delighted.' He then pointed out that in any preliminary examination I might be asked to take, some knowledge of either Latin or Greek would be necessary, and he offered to coach me in whichever I decided to take. As with the music, I was not alight with enthusiasm, and I certainly felt no 'call' or sense of vocation in that direction. Time passed and nothing more came of the idea.

Nevertheless, I was involved in church life as chorister, occasional organist and bell-ringer, and because there was no drinking-water anywhere near the church, I was given the simple duty of taking a bottle of water from home on Sunday mornings for the eight o'clock celebration of the Holy Communion. I carried it in my pocket in one of those once-familiar medicine bottles graduated in tablespoons, and it was always sufficient for the number of communicants present. The collection at this service was taken by the vicar for his 'Poor Fund', which he distributed, half a crown here, a shilling there, among the poor of the parish, widows always having first claim on his meagre funds.

I thoroughly enjoyed carrying out simple duties around the church, including stoking the giant 'Tortoise' stove which stood at the back of the church, its top sometimes glowing red-hot. Very occasionally I pumped the organ, when the regular 'blower' failed to turn up. There was a strange fascination about that little lead weight as it rose and fell on its length of string, and an almost irresistible temptation to allow it to pass the ominous 'bellows empty' mark simply to see what would happen.

One Christmas Eve – I believe it was 1928 – I joined my fellow bell-ringers at the church at six p.m., when we 'raised' the bells and left them ready for ringing. There was no late-night service in the church, so we 'rang in' Christmas Day from midnight until nearly one o'clock. Snow was falling steadily when I left home, and it continued falling throughout the evening, a thick but gentle fall of large, feathery flakes. We spent the evening touring the village with a set of twelve handbells and collecting money we shared out later. This custom gave the parishioners an opportunity of showing their appreciation of our services at the church, calling the faithful and the unfaithful to worship week by week throughout the year, and we did not feel bound to limit our calls to church-goers only.

Snow had stopped falling, but the streets lay under three or four inches of it when we set off for the church later in the evening. We were all present, sober and ready at the appointed time, and at the signal, 'Here goes', about one minute past midnight, we pulled off, one after the other. To our surprise and mystification, no sound followed; there was no joyful response from the bells. At first, only silence, then a muffled, far-away sound from one or two bells only. For a moment or two something of the awe and magic of Christmas seemed to fill the ringing-chamber. Then, one by one, the silent bells found their tongues, and we realized that, while standing mouth upwards for five or six hours, they had filled with snow which had drifted in through the louvres during our absence. The explanation seemed too simple to account for such an unusual occurrence, particularly at the hour of midnight on a cold, snowy Christmas Eve.

We did very little handbell-ringing on Christmas Day, as most of the ringers preferred to be with their families, but we made a full day of it on Boxing Day. At most doors we were received warmly and rewarded generously; at some we were asked inside to entertain the company with a selection from our repertoire of carols, hymns and songs – one gentleman said he thought 'Little Brown Jug' was a much better tune than 'The First Nowell'. Nearly all pressed us to have 'a glass of wine and a mince pie', until of wine and mince pies we were heartily, and almost literally sick, – but how could we be so ungracious as to refuse? Besides, we weren't forgetting that half a crown or perhaps even a 10-shilling note might come our way before we left.

At one house Bill, our captain, knocked hard on the back door, then motioned us to follow him. Trooping in we found ourselves in a large, flagstoned kitchen with a scrubbed table in the centre, also bare except for a cup and saucer and an empty plate. An old man with a small, completely bald head sat in a high-backed chair near the fire. He seemed pleased to see us, and Bill asked him what he would like us to play, but he either didn't know any carols or hymns or didn't care what we played. However, we shuffled into position and gave him a couple of tunes. When we had finished, he smiled and nodded his head, and this we took as a signal for more. When we next paused, he seemed to recollect himself and fumbling in his pocket produced a florin (2 shillings) and put it on the table in front of us. We agreed to play again, although the old chap seemed to be dozing rather than listening, and as soon as we had finished we filed quietly out.

'I thought we'd give the old chap a treat and brighten his day,' Bill said. The florin still lay on the table.

In one of the crowded public houses a round of cold roast beef stood at one end of the bar and a good-sized ham at the other, along with a plentiful supply of pickled onions. Regulars and casuals alike were served generously with the meat of their choice.

At the 'Grand Dance' held on Boxing Day, all ages from eight to eighty enjoyed varied, lively dancing until the early hours, declaring, as they stepped out of the brightly lit hall into the darkness of the unlit street, that they had had a wonderful time; and tired or not, the men would be at work at seven o'clock the next morning.

We finished handbell-ringing at the vicarage on New Year's Eve at the invitation of the vicar and Mrs Aylwin. A cold supper was provided, with plenty of beer and cigarettes for those who wanted them, and a 10-shilling note went into our kitty. The choir were entertained about a week later. The general opinion was that the new parson was 'a decent sort of chap'.

After the share-out, it was off to church again to ring out the old year and ring in the new. With a little over £2 in my pocket I felt exceedingly rich, and at a nod from the captain would have continued ringing till daybreak.

8

We plough the fields

Much of the straw we produced on our newly ploughed land was used for thatching, while the rest provided valuable bedding.

My contribution to the thatching was the making of 'prickers' – our name for thatching-pegs, which were usually made of willow. Most of the willow trees growing near the rickyard had been allowed to grow away and were as tall as the nearby elms, but two or three had been pollarded regularly to provide us with prickers. A 'chopping-block', a bill-hook and a sharp knife for trimming one end of the prickers to a point were the only tools I needed. The work, though somewhat tedious, was satisfying, and the whiteness of the freshly cut wood had something fascinating about it and was always pleasing to the eye.

The thatch was held in place with tarred twine stretched between the pegs and tied tightly round the top of each peg before it was thrust home, as far into the stack as it would go. When twine ran out, we twisted long ropes of hay to replace it. The ideal material was long, tough hay which could be twisted tightly into a strong rope without breaking or falling apart. To toughen it, we usually splashed water on it before we started. The tool we used for the job was very like a car starting-handle with a hook at the end. Hay bonds were often used to tie up trusses of hay but were never wasted – they were shaken out and thrown down with the rest of the truss for the cattle to eat. Our amusingly primitive methods were

efficient and cheap, and some of the materials we used repro-
duced themselves on the farm and didn't cost us a penny.

Before thatching was finished, preparations for the next
year's harvest were already under way, with some ploughing
done. One year Dad said he thought it was about time I put my
hand to the plough. My first attempts at the ancient craft
proved a rude awakening – it had always looked so easy, but
when I took the plough handles and the horses moved off, I got
a nasty shock. The plough, until that moment an inanimate
object, suddenly sprang to life in my hands and became a living
creature with a temper and will of its own. Before we had
travelled half a dozen yards, it turned sharply to the right
without the slightest warning and ran out into the furrow.
After what seemed like a desperate struggle with a monster, I
eventually succeeded in getting it back to roughly where I
wanted it, but before I could get it on an even keel, the other
wheel climbed slowly out of the furrow to the right, and I
found myself ploughing two feet wide. Then, when I thought I
was getting the hang of it, the tip of the share struck a stone or
some silly obstruction, and the plough leapt clean out of the
furrow and fell on its side. The plough had taken the first
round. Meanwhile, Dad, holding the horses, pointed back
along the furrow at the crooked mess I'd made, and shook his
head in despair. Ploughing a straight furrow was harder than I
had expected; it was certainly much harder than it looked.

Nevertheless, with experience and with the plough correctly
set and under complete control, ploughing was satisfying and
enjoyable, though very tiring. I no longer gripped the handles
as tightly as before; indeed, there were times when they
required only the lightest touch, but I could still feel the share
nosing and crunching its way along, cutting and lifting the soil
which the mouldboard turned slowly over, leaving a dark,
lengthening ribbon of freshly turned earth behind me. Though
I never did reach the advanced stage of being able to handle
both plough and horses, I have always been able to appreciate
and admire the consummate skill of the true ploughman.

The house and field in the village had both been part of the
estate of Sir Gerald Shuckburgh, Bt, and although we had
bought the house we still received demand notes around Lady

Day (25 March) and Michaelmas Day (29 September) for the rent of the sixteen-acre field, requesting that it be paid at the forthcoming rent audit at 'the Hall'.

A helpful gesture on the part of the landlord was to hold the spring audit in May, thus allowing tenants to get their cattle into saleable condition after the winter, and purchasers to be able to put the animals straight into a good bite of grass where they would require no further hand-feeding. The autumn audit was held in November, when tenants might reasonably be expected to have fattened off lambs and beef cattle and to have cashed their harvest.

If Dad were busy, and probably thinking the experience might be useful to me, he would send me off to Shuckburgh, some two or three miles away, with a cheque in my pocket. Tenants went into the office one at a time to pay their rent and to meet the landlord and his agent, who were there to listen to moans and grievances and to discuss problems as well as collect the rent.

But the day was also a pleasant social occasion, with a good dinner and a plentiful supply of beer. The huge joint of beef at the head of the table was from one of the tenants' own animals, and before carving the first slice the landlord would make a little speech, to which a senior tenant would reply. I was somewhat over-awed by the all but silent butler; nevertheless, I thoroughly enjoyed myself, and when the footman offered me a second helping of treacle tart, I didn't refuse it.

A few of the more prosperous-looking tenants hurried away as soon as they had completed their business, not even staying for dinner – they were busy men, and there was work to be done on the farm. Most took advantage of the opportunity for a chat with their cronies over an after-dinner drink. Those who were there when I left said they were staying until all the beer had gone.

One feudal-like condition was attached to tenancy agreements. In the autumn a boat-load of coal was moored at the wharf in Shuckburgh village, and tenants undertook to haul this winter's supply of fuel from the wharf to the cellars at the Hall. It was a haul of about a mile, but nearly half that distance was up a long and fairly steep incline.

Since those distant times farming fortunes have swung full circle. In post-war years landlords refused to rent out land at any price, much preferring to take it in hand and farm it themselves.

Despite the deepening depression of the late twenties, Dad found the money to invest in a brand-new hay-loader, a machine which collected hay from the row, conveyed it up a short elevator and dumped it on the wagon. It was a wonderful tool, but it made dusty, exhausting and frustrating work for the poor fellow trying to build the load. By rights, two horses and two men were needed to cope with this punishing task, but such a strong force was seldom available, and consequently the era of the hay-loader spanned only a few years.

The new machines coming onto farms were still horse-drawn, and the animals had a bad time of it – more work, harder work and even longer hours. Sore shoulders were a common affliction, and relief was often given by fixing a pad under the collar, where it would take pressure off the sore. Stockholm tar was widely used for dressing wounds and sores, and stiff mud was sometimes daubed on as a temporary means of keeping off tormenting flies.

Sunday brought a brief respite from labour for man and horse, for as yet no work was done on that day other than the tending of livestock. It was good to see the horses standing head to tail in the shade of the trees, the tail of one conveniently swishing the flies from the head of its companion. Many farmers, including my father, took a leisurely walk round the farm on Sunday morning. There was time for a careful appraisal of cattle and lambs fattening on the pasture, and time to make an up-to-the-minute assessment of hay and corn crops. Neighbours would gossip over a gate or stile, probably comparing notes while the distant murmur of church bells summoned parishioners to worship.

The farmer leaning on a gate, the folk gathered together in church, and the horses resting under the trees were all, in their different ways, aware that Sunday was a special day, offering them a pause in the week's occupations, good for man and beast.

When the vicar asked me whether I would like to read a lesson in church one Sunday evening, I was thrilled to death. Not since the day I had been asked to recite my piece, 'The Slave's Dream', on stage in Junior School at the end of term had I had an opportunity of exhibiting myself and my skill in public. I was now old enough to realize that reading in church was an important and responsible duty, and I was a little apprehensive.

The vicar's unexpected request immediately reminded me of my first visits to church with my mother, listening to Parson John's powerful voice. One Sunday he was reading from Isaiah 55 when some words caught my attention, and for the first time I found myself listening – listening to the music of words. The reader was a tall, large-chested man, and these words rolled from his lips and boomed across the church: 'For my thoughts are not your thoughts, neither are your ways my ways, saith the Lord.' Years later I noticed that of the sixteen words in this sentence only one contains more than one syllable. Simplicity and beauty can go together.

The lesson I was given to read was the parable of the Prodigal Son, from Luke 15, and I was afraid I might fail to do it justice.

A more regular duty was to help with the bells, and when the ringers failed to turn up, the verger and I chimed the five bells between us, he pulling three ropes, and I the other two.

The gentle sound of bells being properly chimed is more restful and, to some, more pleasing to the ear than the louder, harsher sound of ringing which, unless done with reasonable skill, can produce a nerve-jangling cacophony.

Newcomers to a village where the bells are rung regularly sometimes begin complaining about the noise before they have been in the place more than five minutes, and so ill-feeling soon arises between the newcomer and the ringers, and sometimes between the newcomer and the incumbent of the parish. This sort of thing is regrettable, but it could be avoided if estate agents took the trouble to make enquiries about the bells when they are trying to sell a property near a village church – they should find out whether the bells are rung, at what times they are rung and for how long at a session, and be sure to pass on any relevant information to prospective buyers. Even so, when people purchase a property 'delightfully situated near the picturesque village church', they must expect to take what goes with it.

On practice night, usually one evening a week, the novice strives to become proficient, the proficient more proficient, but the slightest mistake usually results in a loud, discordant clang. Without the tolerance and understanding of those living nearby, bell-ringing would be impossible in many places.

Clergy and ringers are well aware that a noise problem can arise, and the authorities have experts available to give advice. I have personally helped to hump concrete blocks, one at a time, up a narrow, spiral, stone stairway into the ringing-chamber. These blocked off a considerable area occupied by open louvres through which the sound of the bells had rung out for centuries.

During the long winter evenings, with nothing to do and nowhere to go, I became bored and restless. I posted off articles and stories to editors of newspapers and magazines, and in time collected a small sackful of rejection slips, but not a line did I sell. That I had been denied the opportunity of sitting for School Certificate probably added to my discontent. I could see that the possession of this document opened doors to my contemporaries which would always be closed against me.

Thus it was that I enrolled with a correspondence college for a course in five School Certificate subjects. I realized that I was at a considerable disadvantage in having no equipment available for help in any of the practical subjects, and that oral coaching in a foreign language would also be unobtainable. Nevertheless, from the limited number of subjects at my disposal I selected five and set to work, swotting away after the family had gone to bed.

The examination took place in July 1929, at Daventry Grammar School, where I was warmly received by everybody. There was a warm, friendly atmosphere about the place, and I felt relaxed and quite at home the moment I crossed the threshold. Unfortunately we were busy haymaking at the time, and the thought of going off to

Daventry three or four days during the week made me feel terribly uncomfortable. Most of my papers were taken at times which caused little inconvenience at the farm, but the last paper, geography, was set for late afternoon.

The day arrived, fine, hot and sunny – a perfect haymaking day, and we had a quantity of hay almost ready for carting. When the time came, I could not bring myself to 'down tools' and desert the field, and I could not summon up enough courage to remind Dad about my exam. I had never felt so guilty about anything in my life, and after much hesitation and heart-searching I decided to say nothing. I would stay and help with the hay. So time and opportunity slipped away. Then, quite unexpectedly, about mid-afternoon, Dad said, 'I thought you had an exam this afternoon. You'd better get off.' By that time, however, pens were already scratching away in Daventry. Though I should have known better, I was surprised to learn that my father was the least bit interested in my ridiculous schemes. Had he spoken an hour earlier, I would still have hesitated – torn between the all-important hay and half a dozen questions on a piece of paper.

When I got home, I found a telegram from the headmaster of the school saying he was sorry I hadn't turned up for the exam but if I would go in the next morning and take the paper he would do his best to get it off in time. I took the paper the following morning but was told that it was most unlikely my late entry would be accepted.

The Pass List informed me that I had passed in four subjects, including a 'credit' in English; but five passes were required to gain a certificate, so if I decided to try again, I would have to take five subjects again, and to pass in all five at one and the same examination. It was too daunting a prospect for my weak spirit. I gave up.

In my late teens I was still much more squeamish than any farmer's boy should have been, and found many jobs connected with livestock difficult to face. When we had a cow calving and help was needed, I always hung back until I was called to pull on the ropes; and lambing I found equally distasteful, but the one thing I really detested was the knacker-cart with its blood-stained tarpaulin, and the head of horse or beast the sheet did not conceal. Unlikely though it sounds, the knacker's business we had dealings with was carried on by a woman. She was usually accompanied by a man but would sometimes be on her own, and would carry out her ghoulish duties with humane killer and the pulley with which she hauled the carcase onto the cart as though she were enjoying every second. And she was a good-looking young woman to boot.

One day I saw a pullet floundering in a patch of mud. It was obviously too weak to make its way out of the morass, so I picked it up, intending to put it down on clean, dry land, but I discovered that the wretched creature was nothing but skin and bone – a breathing skeleton. Looking at it, I realized that the humane thing to do was to put an end to its suffering as soon and as quickly as possible. I decided to do it myself. Having seen lots of poultry killed (Dad was an expert at it), I had a pretty good idea how to set about the job. I gripped its legs firmly in my right hand, its head in my left, and a moment later I felt the neck break cleanly and quickly. I had carried out a mercy killing, humanely, and had acquired a useful new skill.

Though Dad liked seeing the hens scratching around the farmyard and ranging the fields, they showed little profit, and raids by foxes were a constant risk. During the winter most of the hens were ready to go to roost before we left for the village, and so we were able to feed them in the fowl-house and drop the shutter in the pop-hole, making them safe for the night. But in summer it wasn't so easy, and no amount of whistling and calling could coax them into that stuffy fowl-house at 4.30 on a summer afternoon, so some unlucky member of the family tramped across the fields to shut them up later in the evening, around nine or ten o'clock in the middle of summer.

Then Dad had an idea which he said would cut out the irksome chore. He suspended a chain in the pop-hole, and when the hens became used to it, he added a second; finally three chains, between two and three inches apart, dangled and tinkled in the pop-hole. Much to our surprise, the hens were soon going in and out between the chains without any hesitation, as though unaware of their existence. Dad's theory was that no sensible fox would be rash enough to put its head between those chains; it would be too suspicious of them, fearing a trap, so from then on the hens were left ranging the fields when we went home in the afternoon, and free to go to roost as early or as late as they wished.

For some weeks all went well. Then, one morning, we arrived at the farm to find that a fox had dared to force the magic chains, pushing between them into the fowl-house and slaughtering or maiming most of its helpless inmates. Those left unharmed skulked, terrified and trembling, in corners. Dad collected up the carcases, tossed them into the trap and took them to the hunt kennels, where he was paid a few shillings' compensation for his loss. He was lucky to get anything – few hunts made a practice of paying out on poultry.

The surviving hens suffered badly from shock and stopped laying, while many went into a moult and did not come back into lay until they had grown a new coat of feathers. (Hens laid most of their eggs during the summer, and it was the usual custom to preserve some of these summer eggs for use in the winter. They were preserved by dropping them into a pail containing a sodium silicate solution in which they could be kept for several months and then be used for any purpose.)

There are those who would have us believe that the fox kills only what it needs to satisfy its hunger – sufficient only for its immediate needs. If only that were true! Unfortunately, it is not so.

9

One man went to mow

Young people find it difficult to believe that in the days of the horse and cart rural transport and delivery services of every kind were faster, more readily available and much more reliable than in our high-speed, high-tech era. No one would now dream of delivering a loaf of bread to Mrs Hodges in her cottage at the end of the lane.

The two bakers in our village made crusty, mouth-watering bread which they delivered to the door six days a week. If there was no reply to his knock, within a few seconds the busy baker would step inside and put his warm loaves on the kitchen table. Deliveries to outlying farms and cottages were made three times a week. Cakes were made twice a week but could be made to order at any time.

The two butchers with shops in the village bought their animals at the nearest market or from local farmers, from where they went direct to the slaughterhouse 'on the hoof'. One butcher slaughtered in a shed behind the shop, the other used the shop when it was closed for business. (On certain days of the week that shop had a magnetic fascination for those children tall enough to see over the half-door.) Two other butchers toured the village twice a week with their ponies and spotless, white 'box traps'. Such a keen, competitive service offered everyone the widest possible choice – and, of course, everything was delivered to the door. We country folk must have consumed an awful lot of meat in those days to have made it worthwhile so many butchers competing for our custom.

An ironmonger from Leamington visited the village once a week. His horse-drawn, open-sided shop resembled a good-sized tinker's cart and always carried a surprisingly wide range of goods. Pots and pans, brushes and soaps were but a few of the things he carried; in great demand, especially during the winter, were candles, paraffin and matches. In bad weather an aged or infirm customer had only to open the door and the ironmonger would step inside, take the paraffin can, fill it from the tank slung under his cart and return it along with a new lamp wick, a packet of candles or anything else his customer had asked for. Any article he did not have with him he undertook to deliver the following week, but if it was required urgently, it would be sent out with the carrier, probably next day. Prompt and courteous service – with a horse and cart.

Although there were two good general stores in the village besides two or three old ladies who sold sweets and tobacco, a Leamington store delivered in the village every week. An 'up-market' store delivered to some of the 'big houses' and, in addition to the usual provisions, was able to supply from the delicatessen department and wine cellar such luxuries as china tea, a bit of tasty Gorgonzola cheese or a case of vintage port, but they were few in number who had a taste for such things, and fewer still who could afford them.

On Friday evening or Saturday morning – before wages were spent, outfitters' salesmen called for their 6 pence or shilling a week clothing club subscription. Three of these gentlemen came into the village. Clothing and goods ordered one week were usually delivered the next, and, of course, you could be measured for any garment you wished without leaving the comfort of your own fireside. It goes without saying that articles were altered or exchanged until the customer was completely satisfied.

Mail was delivered twice daily, the second post frequently dropping through the letter-box between five and 5.30 in the afternoon, and a man with a horse and cart collected goods and parcels from the station, where a goods clerk was employed to deal with the business. A gentleman who owned a comfortable governess cart and a four-wheeled wagonette carried passengers to and from any station within reasonable distance, including main-line stations. Anyone wanting the early morning express from Rugby to Euston could be certain of catching it. That's how isolated we were.

But the man who kept us in close touch with the town, who made us feel that the large, town stores were only just round the corner, was the carrier. Without doubt, the local carrier rendered invaluable service to the community he served.

Two carriers worked from Napton: one ran twice weekly to Coventry, and my uncle still ran his family business with a twice-weekly trip to Leamington. On the outward journey they carried eggs, butter and poultry, and there might be something from one of the village shops to be returned or exchanged, and they collected and delivered for all and sundry. On the return journey they might be carrying anything from a bottle of patent medicine to a cumbersome piece of furniture.

Their covered vans could also accommodate up to half a dozen passengers in tolerable comfort, although, with a full complement of passengers and with boxes and parcels stacked around, conditions could be rather cramped until the first passengers or parcels were dropped off along the way. But it was no hardship for the younger passengers, especially if their feet felt like blocks of ice, to step down and walk up the steepest hills. After Saturday morning school in Leamington I occasionally rode home with my uncle in the afternoon, and I remember being sent to a house with a small parcel and instructed to collect 3 pence for its delivery.

Most weeks a large bowl of dripping obtained from one of the hotels in the town was sold in the village for 4 pence a pound. While good beef dripping was more palatable than home-made butter in the winter, Mother bought it so that she could sell all her butter.

It is now possible to jet round the world faster than the speed of sound, yet people living in the country without a bus service and without a car are further from town, less well served and more isolated than we and our parents were over sixty years ago, in the age of the horse and cart.

One summer morning, after playing the saxophone in a dance band until the early hours at a dance in the village some miles away, I arrived home about three o'clock with the sky already showing more than a glimmer of daylight. I knew I was supposed to be making an early start at mowing, so I decided there was little point in going to bed.

At twenty, I was quite capable of handling a pair of horses and the two-horse mowing-machine, so I changed into working-clothes, went to the fields, caught and harnessed the horses and hitched them to the mower. Somewhere between half-past four and five o'clock the first swath was falling away behind me. At that hour, the most beautiful time of day, with the dewdrops on the grasses beginning to glisten in the early morning light, everything smelled fresh and clean, the movement and vibration of the machine were exhilarating, and for a while I didn't feel the least bit tired.

As the horses moved along and the knife chattered through the grass, a dense cloud of multicoloured pollen rose from the ripening grass-heads, but the thought of wearing a mask never entered my head, and since I had never come across anyone who suffered from what was known as 'hay-fever', I ignored the cloud of dust – I suffered no ill effects as a result of my ignorance. Before the sun had completely burnt off the dew, meadow brown butterflies began rising from the grass. Soon they were rising in a continuous dark cloud, disturbed by the mower as it moved through the grass. I had never seen anything quite like it before, nor have I since. That must have been a particularly good year for meadow browns.

At about eight o'clock breakfast was brought into the field for me. The day was already so warm that I decided to eat in the shade of a nearby ash tree, while the horses, their bits removed, helped themselves to fragrant, freshly cut, green grass.

The exhilaration of the first hour had long since worn off, and it was a relief to get away from the clatter of the machine for a while, and from the bone-shaking seat; besides, my arms were aching – controlling and guiding a pair of horses so that the 'heel' of the cutter-bar never strayed out of the foot-wide track between standing grass and newly cut swath was always a muscle-stretching exercise; so I decided to rest for five minutes before eating. Stretching full-length on my back I stared up at the cool, green canopy of motionless leaves spread above me. Larks were filling the sky with song, while nearer at hand a wood-pigeon crooned a soothing lullaby; so soothing was it that when Dad arrived in the field I was fast asleep. He soon had me on my feet, and I heard him muttering something about burning the candle at both ends.

Fagging-hooks were put aside or used only for chopping a way in for the binder, and the home-made reaping-machine was pushed to the back of the barn when a farming cousin set himself up with a Fordson 'Standard' tractor and a Massy-Harris binder – both second hand, of course. It was arranged that he would cut our corn and that we, in return, would give him a hand with his shooking and carting.

A certain amount of skill was required to build shooks that would withstand rough weather, but care was also taken to ensure that they were in line with one another in the rows and that the rows were parallel whatever shape of the field. When finished, a field of wheat or oats, carefully and expertly shooked, was a rewarding and pleasing sight, especially to those who had worked and waited for hope to become reality.

Though we no longer see corn standing in the fields, nor neat, trim ricks adorning the rickyard, the old skill and craftsmanship have not been completely killed off by the machine. The thatcher and hedger still work with their hands, not with a machine, and at the end of the day they can view with pride what those hands have accomplished.

What human hands can accomplish was demonstrated when a large pond on the edge of the village went dry. The pond was less than half a dozen yards off the road and lay parallel with it for a distance of some twenty yards. A traveller could turn off the road and drive through the pond and out onto the road again to continue his journey. This 'drive-through' was common practice in summer, when the wooden wheels of vehicles dried out and spokes and felloes became loose with the risk that iron tyres might fall off and the wheels collapse. When wooden hub, spokes and felloes – the wooden sections forming the rim of the wheel – shrank in dry weather, a slow drive through the pond every few days kept everything tight, and was regarded as good insurance against a collapsed wheel.

Then came the year when the pond dried up and was found

to be chock full of mud and rubbish. It was obvious that it badly needed cleaning out, but no individual would consider tackling such a mammoth task. However, a number of farmers got together, pooled their resources and set about the job in an organized, business-like manner. While a couple of carts went off with a load of spoil, two more were backed into the stone-lined pond to be filled by four or five of us with shovels. With carts moving to and fro continuously and with a team of willing workers in the pond, surprisingly good progress was made. The unprintable remarks made about the pond, the mud and the stink, all in light-hearted vein, made the dirty, smelly job much more tolerable, and time to pass more quickly. A few horses and carts and a few shovels with hands to wield them completed the task in a matter of days.

Co-operation between friends and neighbours was also helpful when cattle were to be taken to market. Pigs, sheep and calves would be taken in trap or float with a net tied over them to prevent escape, but larger animals were driven to market on foot – there was no other way of getting them there.

Two or three farmers driving their cattle together ensured there being enough drovers to keep the cattle together. This was not always easy in winter, when most of the twelve-mile journey to Rugby, our usual market, was made in darkness. To arrive at the market at a reasonable time we usually set out at around 4 a.m., the journey, at easy walking pace, taking a little over four hours.

After seeing the cattle penned and entered in the auctioneer's book, we were ready for some refreshment, and this we obtained at one of the taverns provided mainly for drovers. Old-fashioned places they were – Victorian, perhaps, although we didn't see anything wrong with them, with tiled walls, heavy, marble-topped tables and wooden settles round the walls. In winter a fire burned in the large grate at which we warmed ourselves as we sipped our large mugs of steaming-hot cocoa. The return journey, a more speedy one, was made in the comfort of the trap.

Livestock from a distance travelled to market by rail. Large numbers came over from Ireland to markets such as Banbury and Rugby, situated only yards from a main-line railway station. Farmers who bought them had them delivered by rail, for hardly a country station but had its siding for a few cattle trucks equipped with a convenient loading-bay, and from there it was easy enough to drive either sheep or cattle the final leg of the journey to the farm on foot.

During these years cowslips were still plentiful in their season, and though Dad wasn't usually caught picking flowers, once a year he gathered a good fistful of cowslips. Along with some sweetly scented violets, Mother placed them in a shoebox lined with moss, sprinkled them liberally with water and posted them to Dad's sister in Coventry. Nellie didn't really need flowers, as besides having a large garden she had a husband, a successful builder, who would have bought her a florist's shop had she but whispered the word.

Arthur took a good holiday most years, sometimes abroad, but Nellie seldom accompanied him, much preferring a week or two with her parents at their cottage in Napton. One afternoon she came for a ride with us in the pony and float and on the return journey across the fields asked if she could take the reins. Dad handed them over. Nellie flicked the reins lightly across Kitty's rump, and she immediately broke into a fast trot. The ground was hard and rough, with no grass to serve as a cushion in the bare August pasture, and the old float creaked and rattled as though it were about to fall to pieces at any moment, but Nellie was having the time of her life. I expected her hairpins to fall out and her hair to go flying out behind her as we clattered along. There was a sparkle in her eyes as she finally reined Kitty in – she had probably enjoyed herself that afternoon more than she had done for many a day.

Dad said that Nellie had once come into the harvest field wearing her long, tight town clothes on a very hot day. After only a few minutes she slipped off a heavy petticoat and her knickers (or whatever garment it was they wore those days), threw them aside and continued laying bonds.

Though happily married, with a comfortable home on the outskirts of Coventry, Nellie was a country girl at heart, and when April came she half-expected to be able to go out into the meadow and gather cowslips and to find herself reaching

Jim and Lizzie Barrett,
my grandparents,
enjoying their well-
earned retirement.
c. 1920.

My father Tom seated
on his home-made
reaping machine in
1928. I am standing at
the horse's head.

The Church Army van on Napton village green in 1924. From left to right are shown Captain Forshaw, Captain Peters and Cadet Bullock.

The parish church of St Lawrence, Napton is always open and welcomes visitors to share its tranquillity. The Revd Peter Jackson has been vicar since 1972.

The pond at Chapel Green, Napton, as it was around 1930 – pleasant to look upon and useful to the community.

The old cottage, Magpie Hall, in 1937 with Annie in the doorway and two children, Reg and June, just visible through the fence.

Tom Barrett, churchwarden from 1924 to 1944, with his staff, the symbol of his office.

Napton-on-the-Hill disused windmill. In front, an allotment holder's strip of wheat and, nearer the camera, a strip of potatoes.

Bringing in the sheaves, *c.* 1928. Dad ties a sheaf, brother Vic collects stray straws, my sister Winnie in her cloche hat makes a bond and Mother collects ears of corn.

Rick-making. Dad and I are on the rick while Vic, unloading the hay, is doing his best to get it on to the rick with a long-handled pitchfork.

under the greening hedgerow thorns for the sweetest-smelling violets. That was impossible, but Dad thoughtfully provided the next best thing – a bouquet of fragrant spring flowers in which she could bury her face and recall the meadows she had romped in as a child.

Dad was no naturalist but he was very observant. He would often spot and point out a little owl apparently dozing on the branch of a tree, usually near the trunk and inconspicuous. One spring day he pointed out a wheatear perched on a fence post some distance away, and explained that it would not nest near us: it was simply resting on its journey to its usual breeding-ground. I was thrilled when he showed me a redstart's nest containing a clutch of deep-blue eggs, in an old willow tree.

Less fragrant than the spring flowers and less pleasing to the eye than the birds were the contents of the earth closet. After 'it' had been allowed to accumulate for several months under the hole in the elm-plank seat polished smooth by long use, something had to be done, so the horse was hitched up and the cart backed as near as possible to the pit. Dad then took a shovel and set to work. Fortunately I was never asked to help.

A West Country parson recorded in his diary in the early years of the last century that, one day when haymaking was not possible, he set his men to clean out the 'essential' at the bottom of the garden – the smell had been getting offensive. A summer day – even a dull one with, perhaps, hordes of flies buzzing around – was probably not the best time to stir things up with a shovel. Sanitary conditions at the vicarage seem to have been as primitive as they were at the labourers' cottages.

10

Awake, awake, to love and work

The young lady was busy behind the ice-cream stall at a garden fête in the summer of 1930 when I first clapped eyes on her. She was comfortably built, with dark hair and a pair of captivating brown eyes, and I soon discovered that her name was Annie and that she was a farmer's daughter.

Her home was a very remote farmhouse approachable only across six or seven fields – fields she had had to cross daily a few years previously to go to school. When she was three years old she lost her mother, a victim of TB. Her father gamely kept the family together until he too died during the severe post-war flu epidemic. From the age of eleven she was brought up by her grandparents, and when she left school she went into domestic service, returning home to keep house at the farm on the death of her grandmother. Annie could bake bread, make butter, salt a pig, pluck and dress poultry and make pork pies with the best of them. For wages, she received board-and-lodging only, while for pocket-money she did dressmaking in the little spare time she had. When I met her, she had recently bought a small poultry-house out of her savings, with the idea of making a few shillings for herself producing eggs to sell locally, but before she could produce the eggs, she had to produce the poultry.

In her first year she succeeded in rearing nearly thirty pullets to 'point of lay', all hatched under borrowed broody hens. They had reached the stage, bright red of comb and sleek of feather, and the first eggs could be expected any day when, to her surprise, no pullets came running to meet her at feeding-time one misty autumn afternoon. A moment later, coming across bunches of feathers scattered around, she feared the worst. Nearer the fowl-house she found many of her precious pullets lying dead, while others were lying around helpless, with terrible injuries. Only a few had escaped the merciless killer. Annie said that she was so shocked and distressed at what she saw that she burst into tears, and she was still very upset when she told me all about it several days later. The havoc and suffering one fox can cause in a ten-minute raid on a flock of free-range poultry is impossible to describe – it has to be seen to be believed.

It was a bitter disappointment for her. A whole year's work had been completely wiped out, together with the hopes and expectations that had gone with it; but hope springs eternal, and the very next year Annie set to work again, putting eggs under broody hens, tending the chicks and watching them grow and thrive under her care. Her reaction to misfortune was that of the real farmer: he expects to get knocked flat on his back occasionally but, like the wounded soldier, he says, 'I lay me down and bleed awhile, then get me up and fight again.'

Annie and I were married in 1934, and I threw in my lot with my bride's family on what was a bigger farm than Dad's and which, it was thought, offered some scope for a young son-in-law and his wife.

When I joined the family, butter was still being made and retailed locally in the little town of Southam, on the A425, between Leamington and Daventry. Heavy traffic on this road and on the A423 Coventry – Banbury road now thunders through the centre of the town. In a more leisurely age I had stood near the windmill and watched the giant sails and listened to their squeaking and creaking as they turned slowly round and round above my head.

Delivering the butter on a Friday evening made a pleasant change after working on the farm. The customers were a friendly lot, and despite hard times, most of them paid for their butter on the spot. One old lady had had a standing order for a quarter of a pound for years, costing her 6 pence a week during the winter, and 3 pence during the summer. Through the winter, when the cows were fed poor-quality food, it was difficult to fulfil regular orders; in summer, when the cows were on rich, young grass, output increased dramatically, but demand for our product did not.

For several weeks one summer we salted down the surplus in large stone jars for use during the winter, when we found it more palatable than the insipid 'fresh' butter, and it was delicious on toast. Then the time came when we had filled every available jar, yet there was still a quantity of the stuff standing, unsold, on the cold slab in the dairy. We decided to try our luck with it in Banbury market. The weather was very hot, so we wrapped the butter, twenty pounds of it, in large, cool cabbage leaves and hoped we would succeed in selling it before it turned to oil and ran through the bottom of the basket. A butter mountain, even a very small one, can be a headache for those trying to get rid of it.

At the entrance to the produce market we met a man leaving, his face as long as a wet week, and he obviously guessed our errand. 'Don't take it in there, young fellow,' he said. 'They're giving it away – 6 pence a pound I got. I should try the shops.'

We took his advice and retraced our steps into town. The grocery and dairy shops we tried had all the butter they needed – none would take another pound. Then, over a confectioner's shop with a tea-room at the front, we spotted a sign. 'Banbury cakes, made with fresh butter,' it said. I pushed my way through the crowded tea-room into the bakery at the rear and set my basket down very carefully on the table. The baker guessed what was in it and said, without examining the contents, 'A shilling a pound.' He removed the pats of butter very gingerly, counted them and then handed me a £1 note. Butter was on a buyer's market that day. We bought a few Banbury cakes in the shop, and we felt quite proud of ourselves as we ate them, reflecting that next day the shop would be selling Banbury cakes made with our 'fresh butter', even if it wasn't quite as fresh as it might have been.

The saxophone I had enjoyed playing in the dance band cost me £14; I now sold it back to the same shop in Coventry for £4, and adding to that sum almost every penny I possessed

I bought a lovely strawberry-roan Shorthorn cow for £14. She was a friendly, docile creature with a nicely shaped udder, and I walked her slowly home without the slightest difficulty.

I paid about the same for Strawberry as my father would have paid for a similar cow before the 1914 – 18 war, and my great-grandfather in 1850.

For my first weaner pig I had paid over 30 shillings; now, a few years later, when we had a litter to sell, best-quality weaners were making only 15 shillings each, and small ones sometimes made as little as 10 shillings. Farmers were still having a very difficult time, though arable farmers were doing slightly better. Wheat prices were still low – between 20 and 25 shillings a quarter, but under the quota system some subsidies were being paid.

About two years after our marriage the domestic and business arrangements we had made for living and working together began to go wrong, and Dad was quick to notice that all was not well. I stood quite shamefaced in front of him when he put the question directly to me, and I waited for him to say, 'I told you so', but he, in his mature wisdom, made no such comment. Instead, he suggested that we could, if we wished, move into the empty cottage in the fields. I thought it was a stupid idea, but Annie, who had never set eyes on the place in her life, was all for it – she simply wanted to know how long it would take to make it fit to live in.

We began work in November 1936, and a raw, cold month it was. Dad and brother Vic, pitched in and gave all the help they could. Calling in the professionals was out of the question. 'Do-it-yourself' is as old as the hills.

Thick, freezing fog persisted throughout the day and seemed to go on for weeks. It clothed the hedges and trees in a mantle of hoar-frost, and as we crossed the fields to and from work, cattle and sheep, looking ten times their normal size, loomed up before us like shadowy monsters from another world.

For the first few days I could not accept that I was actually going to live in this God-forsaken place. My youthful dreams and aspirations had taken me along more pleasant ways to work in more exciting, more congenial surroundings. The

gloomy weather was quite depressing and probably
accounted to some extent for my complete lack of
enthusiasm. Then, as the days passed, it gradually dawned on
me that I should be pleased at the prospect, certainly not
miserable – I was coming home. The fields out there had been
my playground, and they would soon be my children's
playground, and when spring came, they would again be
bright with daisies; swallows would be twittering on the ridge
of the barn and swooping in and out of the cowshed to feed
their young. My spirits began to revive, and very soon I
found myself looking forward to returning to familiar
surroundings.

While we ate our sandwiches at midday, sitting round a
good fire in the rusty old grate in the living-room, the main
topic of conversation was, inevitably, the new king's
determination to marry an American-born divorcée, Mrs
Wallis Simpson. As this throne-shaking drama moved to its
climax, plastering, paper hanging and painting went quietly
forward at the cottage, soon to become our castle.

No electrician was needed, and since there was neither sink
nor tap in the house, nor even a pump in the yard, no plumber
was required. The work was completed in a matter of weeks,
and at the beginning of December we decided that the house
was ready for us. At that time the local council took little
interest in our goings-on, and no inspectors came nosing
round to scrutinize our workmanship.

Moving-day, in mid-December, turned out to be mild and
sunny; though a fresh, south-west wind had blown away all
traces of frost and fog, it had brought a considerable amount
of rain with it, and every hollow and every rut was now
awash with water. The naked trees, silhouetted against the
blue sky and reflecting in every pool and puddle, looked
freshly washed in the December sunshine.

With our few belongings stacked on the four-wheeled
trolley and securely roped, I set off on my five-mile
migration, the last mile across muddy, rain-sodden fields. The
going was so soft that I was forced to make a detour before I
found a track on which the wheels would travel without
sinking in to their axles and making the task too much for the
straining, sweating horse.

With our infant son and baby daughter in the pram, Annie set off by a more direct route, although the muddy fields still had to be crossed – there was no escaping them. For much of the time the pram wheels were clogged with mud and refused to turn, but her determination and physical strength finally brought her to the cottage. I expected her to be furious with me for bringing her to such an awful place but, much to my surprise, she was neither angry nor disappointed. With the cottage she was well pleased. She had got what she wanted – her own cave and her offspring under her sole care.

We woke next morning to the sound of water running from a land drain into a tank in the yard. Though thick and muddy after heavy rain, it was usually crystal-clear, and it never entered our heads that it might not be fit to drink until it had been boiled.

We moved to the cottage with three milking cows, three calves, one in-pig sow and around fifty head of poultry. Both hens and pullets were upset by the move and laid no eggs till February.

About a month before we moved I had noticed an interesting advertisement in the local paper: the vicar of Priors Marston, in whose parish we would be living, was asking for an organist for whose services a small honorarium would be paid. I hadn't touched an organ for three or four years, except on one occasion. Back in January the vicar of Napton had asked me to play at the memorial service being held for King George V, who had died a few days previously, the regular organist being unable to get time off from his work.

In a moment of rashness I wrote off applying for the post of organist at Priors Marston, and received a reply asking me to call at the vicarage. I called as requested, and after a short interview the vicar took me along to the church – the moment of truth had come. The organ was a small pipe organ with a wooden handle at the side for pumping the bellows, but it also had pedals, like the American organ we had at home, for the organist to use when no 'blower' was available. Probably to satisfy himself that I could manage the instrument on my own, he asked me to use the pedals.

It was a raw November day, and the church icy cold, but

my hands sweated while I waited to be put through the hoop.
The vicar produced the service sheet for the forthcoming
Sunday, and we began by going through a couple of verses of
each of the hymns. Then came the canticles and finally all the
psalms appointed for the day in the psalter, and to the chants
'as set'; of course, all were from the good old *Cathedral
Psalter*. John Woodman, the grey-haired, quietly spoken
vicar, seemed quite satisfied' with my performance and
informed me on the spot that the post was mine if I cared to
take it, and that the honorarium mentioned in the
advertisement amounted to £12 per annum.

I took up my duties as organist at St Leonard's Church on
the last Sunday in November (St Andrewstide) 1936,
following choir practice on the previous Thursday evening.
One of the hymns we sang that day was the St Andrew's
hymn, 'Jesus calls us', another hymn with a heart-stirring
appeal whose words have remained with me through the
years. There were three boys and half a dozen young ladies in
the choir, and the weekly choir practice was always attended
by the vicar, who conducted the music. Thus began my
association with the church and village of Priors Marston
which, except for a break during the war, extended over forty
years.

John Woodman also held the living of nearby Priors
Hardwick, a smaller parish, though its church, St Mary's, is
regarded as the 'mother church'. Both 'Priors' were once part
of the estate of the wealthy Benedictine priory at Coventry.

The vicar of Priors Marston and his neighbour, the vicar of
Napton, had been on friendly terms for some years until the
latter retired, and they usually exchanged pulpits once or
twice a year during the summer. John Woodman, in black suit
and shovel hat, mounted his large, heavy bicycle and cycled
round the lanes to Napton, while Parson John of Napton,
also in black clerical suit and shovel hat, set off across the
fields, following the footpath between the two villages and on
his way passing within a hundred yards of Magpie Hall, from
where Dad had seen him striding out on a summer Sunday
evening.

A more regular user of the two-mile-long footpath was the
saddler from Priors Marston who spent one day a week

repairing horse harness in a little shed in Napton, returning home in the evening loaded with work he could do only at home. People used the footpaths regularly as they went about their business – it was so much quicker than going round by the road. They used the footpaths to save their weary legs and for no other reason.

From the cottage, the village could be reached only by crossing fields. Though the walk of nearly a mile to Priors Marston was pleasant enough in summer, on winter nights, crossing muddy fields in complete darkness without moon or star or friendly, familiar tree-top silhouetted against the sky to guide me, the journey was less pleasant. In foggy weather I was relieved to hear the bells begin, the sound was reassuring, and the direction from which the sound came helped to keep me in the right way. Occasionally, when the bells started again after a break, the sound seemed to be coming from quite the wrong direction, thus warning me that I was off course on my way across the fog-bound field.

On still, frosty nights when the whole dome of the sky was studded with a million stars, I felt as though I wanted to stand and stare in wonder – and sometimes I did. Though I was quite alone, I never, ever, felt lonely or afraid. The brightly lit, noisy streets of the town are a frightening nightmare compared with the tranquillity, the peace and even the sense of security I felt with only the fields and the stars – the wondrous works of God – for company. The only sound I was likely to hear was the cough of a sheep or the grunt of a beast as it slumped down to begin chewing its cud.

After Christmas, the gradually lengthening days, and the first signs of spring were greeted with relief and pleasure. Such simple things as the first glimpse of a celandine open to the sun on the sheltered side of the hedge, or the sound of the blue tit's cheery, tinkling song, was enough to warm the heart and give the spirits a joyous lift. Trivial, perhaps, but welcomed with a delight few town-dwellers would under-stand. They, poor dears, have been led to believe that spring has arrived whenever they see a picture of a newly-born lamb on television or in a newspaper, supplied by a zealous young photographer or reporter determined to be first with the 'scoop'. Farmers have long known that the highest prices for lamb are obtained in the spring, and a few lambs for the Easter market were generally considered to be a worthwhile exercise, though, of course, extra care and feeding were necessary. Lambs born in December and January are not a novelty, nor are they a sign that spring has arrived – indeed, that early lamb shown on television might well be the product of science. Artificial stimulation of the female and artificial insemination make lambing less dependent on Nature and the seasons, though these methods are not likely to be widely used while grass continues to produce the cheapest and best lamb.

11

I learned it in the meadow's path

We were now the third generation setting out to build a future from humble beginnings. Besides making a living, we also aimed to rear some young cattle to enable us to take a few acres of land on our own as soon as possible. It would be tough going, but while we had milk, butter, bacon, potatoes and an egg or two we were not likely to starve. We bought a few loaves of bread each week and augmented them with home-made.

To make the bread, we bought wheat which we ground into flour in our neighbour's mill powered by a petrol engine. Though the flour would not have passed as high-grade bread flour, and grinding it was a slow business, the bread, made with either soda or yeast, was delicious. The coarse bran left after the flour had been sieved we ate as a breakfast cereal. We were eating home-grown bran nearly fifty years ago. It was certainly much too good to feed to pigs and poultry. Incidentally, the oven in the old range left behind in 1916 baked everything perfectly.

Soon after we moved in, Dad tactfully pointed out that with extra livestock and a second family to feed off the one holding we would need more than his present two acres of arable. He also pointed out that his two horses were getting rather long in the tooth and could not be expected to do more than they were already doing; then he made the surprising suggestion that we go mad and buy a tractor rather than replace the horses.

Through an advertisement in a farming magazine we bought a 1932 Fordson 'Standard' for £45. I contributed £17. 10s. towards the cost, paid in small sums spread over several months. We learned that the machine had worked in East Anglia, and we soon discovered that its previous owner had had his money's worth out of it; nevertheless, with this new source of power we hoped to plough up a further four acres of pasture.

We found a tractor plough hiding behind a barn a few miles away. The owner said he wanted a fiver for it but settled for £3, and because the tractor was not fitted with road wheels, we hitched it behind the float and towed it home, its iron wheels clattering along the road as we went.

At first we had only a motley collection of five-gallon oildrums for fuel storage, and when there was a delay in getting them refilled, we didn't hesitate to fill up the tractor's fuel tank with lamp oil. It gave out a dense cloud of filthy, black smoke, had a vile smell and very quickly fouled up the plugs, but we were not fussy about what went into the tank provided it kept the engine running and the wheels turning.

The extra four acres were eventually ploughed and sown with 'Gartons' 60', a red wheat much talked about among corn-growers and seed merchants at that time. It cropped extremely well, turning out a tremendous crop of straw, though corn yield was disappointing. In some parts of the field the shooks were five feet high. The pastures had been heavily stocked for several years, and Dad said we had too much nitrogen in the soil, and not enough phosphate. The crop was much too bulky for the binder to cope with, so we mowed it off with the grass-mower and tidied it up as best we could, into bundles rather than sheaves.

The only time my father had felt anything approaching loneliness at the farm had been at dusk on a winter afternoon, he used to tell us, and during my first winter there I discovered for myself what he had meant. As dusk fell on a short, grey winter afternoon, it was impossible not to notice an almost eerie silence settling over the fields. Sounds that had spoken of life and activity during daylight hours gradually ceased as darkness fell. The distant, unmistakable sound of children escaping from school, the blacksmith's hammer ringing as clear as a bell on his anvil, and the 'chop-chop' of the hedge-cutter's billhook – one by one, all fell silent, and an air of solitude wrapped itself round the lonely cottage. The almost unearthly quiet, the feeling of being suddenly cut off from the outside world, strange though it was, had nothing sinister or frightening about it. On the other hand, rush-hour in the city, just about beginning, would have scared me to death. I had no train to catch, no milling, shoving crowds to contend with, yet I don't suppose I appreciated the fact that I was miles away from such madness and all that ignoble strife.

Dusk, though, had sounds of its own. Some creature, probably a blackbird, hunting a late meal among the leaves under the hedge, seemed to be making a frightful din, while the sudden clamour made by a cock pheasant disturbed on his perch or flying up to his nightly roosting-place was as startling as an unexpected shot from a gun. Inside the house, with the wooden shutters secured across the windows, keeping them frost-free, all was snug and warm. With logs blazing in the grate, and the kettle singing on the hob, we, like the children asleep upstairs, felt secure.

Our first Christmas was a quiet and simple one, and while none of the food was rich – except perhaps the pork pies, it was plentiful and satisfying. Indulgent grandparents and kindly aunts and uncles saw to it that the children had plenty of toys to play with; even so, it looked as though we would be lacking that centre-piece of every home at Christmas – a Christmas tree. Then, walking through the churchyard on Christmas Eve, I spotted a pile of evergreens, probably lopped from branches of trees overhanging the footpath. I sorted through the pile and eventually found a piece I hoped would make a passable Christmas tree.

It was a poor specimen, unlike any Christmas tree you ever saw, but after we had adorned it with a few brightly coloured baubles and tied on half a dozen sugar mice and some small bags of sweets, it looked quite attractive. The children could not have been more delighted had we paid £5 for it; nor would they have been interested in learning where it came from, so we didn't bother to tell them that Daddy had nicked it from the churchyard.

A quiet, uneventful Christmas. I spent as much time as possible with the children, but besides tending my few livestock I had to trudge across the fields a few times to play 'O Come, All ye Faithful' and 'The First Nowell'.

After a few days in the fantasy-world interlude of Christmas we landed back in the real world with a nasty bump. Our bank passbook arrived, and written out carefully by hand with a good old-fashioned pen it showed us that we had a credit balance, on 31 December 1936, of 6 shillings exactly, so we decided to postpone the skiing holiday. Unfortunately we had no regular income.

Then February came, the days began to lengthen and the hens began to lay. At first the eggs were few in number and small in size, but towards the end of the month we considered most of them to be saleable, and before we knew where we were, we found ourselves with two dozen waiting to be turned into cash. There remained the small problem of finding somebody to buy them.

Annie said she would take them to Napton and try to sell them at the Co-op. Several inches of snow had fallen a few days previously, followed by severe frost, but despite the rough going across fields and over numerous stiles and ditches, she succeeded in reaching the village without mishap. But there's many a slip, and less than six yards from the shop door she stepped on a small patch of frozen, padded snow and a moment later was lying flat on her back. Beyond a bruise or two she was unharmed, but the eggs, less well upholstered, were not nearly so lucky. The store manager bought the few undamaged ones, and customers from the shop took the rest and insisted on paying something for them – indeed, with the aid of a spoon and a basin, almost all were salvaged, but instead of the 4 or 5 shillings expected for them, Annie received about half a crown, not nearly enough for the groceries she needed. After that bit of beginner's luck, things began to improve. The manager of the Co-op took all the eggs we produced.

We were anxious to obtain more cattle and some land of our own to put them on, but we could see that in the meantime poultry would have to be the main source of income. Then, as spring crept up on us, we began to wonder how we were to obtain the pullets we would need to produce the eggs. Broody hens could not incubate the number we had in mind, nor did we have any other means of producing them. However, our very good neighbours, Jim and Gwen, who lived three fields from us, at a farm as isolated as our own, came to our aid. Anticipating our need, they offered us the loan of an incubator and a brooder. They loaded the machine with 250 eggs, for which they would accept no payment; they supplied the paraffin to run it and kept it at their own farm, where they were able to keep an experienced eye on it and give it twice-daily attention for three weeks. Mr Micawber was right – things do turn up.

The result was surprisingly successful, and we immediately decided we would have our own incubators for the next season. That autumn the vicar of Napton, the Revd Frank Aylwin, gave up poultry-keeping – he said he found it was taking up too much of his time. From his sale we bought a 'Gloucester' incubator which could incubate a hundred eggs at a time and shortly afterwards we picked up a 'Glevum' with a hatching-capacity of 150. The following spring we were able to afford hatching eggs to load them at a cost of 27s. 6d. per hundred from Sydenham Farm on the outskirts of Leamington Spa. The farm, now buried under bricks and mortar and known as the Sydenham Estate, is part residential, part industrial. The incubators were set one at a time to hatch out at intervals of ten to fourteen days. Our plans for rapid expansion were under way.

Spring grass was usually late with us, at an altitude of nearly 600 feet, but when it did arrive, its effect on milk-yield was dramatic. Almost overnight we found ourselves with more milk than our few calves could drink, and Dad suggested we put the surplus in a bucket, carry it to Napton and after cooling it pour it into one of the churns he was sending to the dairy. It was a good idea from our point of view, and although he must have known that by taking our milk and mixing it with his own he would be breaking the terms of his contract with the dairy and with the Milk Marketing Board, he was obviously prepared to take the risk involved. The wholesale price of milk was a little over a shilling a gallon at that time, so the milk we lugged across the fields every day brought in somewhere between £2 and £3 a month.

The winter of 1937 – 38 was dry, with exceptionally low rainfall, and it was followed by an unusually dry spring; then, for once, March provided more than the peck of dust, proverbially worth a king's ransom.

On Saturday the 19th of that month I returned home around midday to find the cottage in flames. Jim, spotting smoke rising above the trees and instinctively sensing trouble, was quickly on the scene, where he found Annie frantically dragging furniture out of the house, two screaming children clinging to her skirts. Dad, who had been working nearby, had dashed off to the village to phone the fire brigade, but by the time it arrived little could be done except damp down a fire almost burnt out.

Owing to the dry weather, water was extremely scarce, and within a matter of minutes the well and every pond within reach of the hoses had been pumped dry. With no more water available, the firemen departed, leaving behind the burnt-out cottage, still smouldering, dangerously near the wooden farm buildings and their contents.

Most of the furniture had been rescued and stacked in the barn, while the incubators, both full of eggs in course of incubation, were put in the yard, the lamps extinguished and the developing chicks left to take their chance. I was just about all in at the end of the day, but I could not bring myself to abandon the incubators as a dead loss even though the eggs were stone-cold, so we found a place for them in a draught-proof corner of the barn. I then lit the lamps, left them to warm up to the correct temperature – and hoped for a miracle. We had been overwhelmed with offers of accommodation, but my parents had empty rooms in their large house, so to them we went, and from there I walked each day to do my chores at the farm.

I tended the incubators twice daily until the normal incubation period had come and gone. Of a chick emerging there was neither sight nor sound, but I continued to turn the eggs regularly and to sprinkle them with water, though with rapidly fading hope. Then one day I was sure I heard a faint 'cheep-cheep'. I was both thrilled and surprised at the sound but knew it was much too early to begin counting. Hatching began slowly and dragged out over several days with both machines, but the final result was a hatch of around a hundred bright-eyed, fluffy chicks from 250 eggs – not good, but by no means a disaster.

The cottage had been kept fully insured down the years, and the insurance company promptly paid out the full sum, £100. This covered the whole cost of restoration.

Our increasing number of livestock still running with my father's became too many for the land to bear in the dry spring of that year, but we were able to buy two fields of valuable summer grazing less than a mile from home for which we paid £3 per acre, where the cattle put on flesh and became sleek of coat. However, in August the owner of the fields informed us that all the ponds had dried up, and we were obliged to bring the stock away.

Hay-making methods had changed dramatically since the twenties. The hay-loader, such an exciting machine when it first appeared on the scene to oust the primitive pitchfork, was itself now obsolete. The hay-sweep became the implement of the day, along with its complement, the elevator, for carrying the hay onto the stack. The horse-sweep and later the tractor-sweep speeded up hay-collection tremendously. A few farmers with more money than sense used a car for sweeping hay – a car could travel even faster than a tractor, and speed was becoming as important on the farm as in the factory. John Peel painted a true picture in his poem 'The Land' when he wrote, 'The haytime is a swift and reeking roar.'

Unfortunately motor cars were neither designed nor constructed for sweeping hay. The radiator grille became clogged with insects, seeds and dust in a very short time, causing the water to boil, and the car with its load of hay piled in front would cross the field enveloped in a dense cloud of steam; and there was always the temptation to fetch in another load before topping up the radiator – often a costly mistake. Most car radiators met their end when one of the long steel-tipped wooden prongs of the sweep which pushed the hay into a heap and then transported it to the shack snapped and pierced the grille. The much-abused hay-sweeping car was an animal doomed to enjoy a very short life, and the number of years it was used were few indeed.

The pre-war years of change, of transition from horse-power to tractor-power, were exciting, and if present-day young farmers could see some of the 'Heath-Robinson', blacksmith-made contraptions we used for converting a horse-drawn machine to tractor-drawn, they would howl with laughter. Whether an up-to-date, conscientious Health and Safety Inspector would have been amused is another matter, for there is no doubt we often risked serious injury, or worse, but agricultural implement manufacturers were soon turning out a wide range of implements specially designed for the tractor. The horse age had come to an end – we were now in the machine age. And didn't we know it?

Before we had been the proud owners of a tractor for more than a few weeks, we discovered that we had to learn a new language: to the vocabulary of the horse-keeper we added that of the motor mechanic. The tractor gave us quite a bit of trouble, and like most machines of its day it was always difficult to start in cold weather. Dad would look on, fuming with impatience, while my brother and I stood breathless, our tongues hanging out after a long spell at the starting-handle. 'The horses would have finished the job by now,' he would say in disgust, and I wouldn't have been surprised to see him lay about that tractor with his walking-stick. Other troubles with it compelled us to acquire a fair amount of mechanical skill. At different times over a period of a couple of years we fitted big-ends and piston rings, and with the tractor stripped down in the middle of the field we fitted a new roller-bearing in the gear-box.

Our third child, a daughter, was born in September 1938 while we were still living with my parents, and the cottage, fully restored, was ready for occupation in November. Doting grandparents, however, tried hard to persuade us to stay with them until the spring. We agreed to stay until after Christmas, and then, on a bitterly cold January day, we packed our bags and returned to the cottage. We must have been mad. That the walls had not thoroughly dried out and that it was unheated didn't worry us one bit – we were home again. Today, under such conditions, an over-zealous social worker would have had the children taken from us and put 'in care'.

During our absence rats and mice had also been busy producing families. Despite the cats around, they seemed to have made good use of the months we had been away, leaving them undisturbed to breed and multiply, but though house and barn were part of the same building, mice rarely appeared in the house, and rats never.

One night in the spring, on my last round of the chick-brooders, I was startled by a large rat scuttling from under a brooder and disappearing into the hedge. That rat spelt danger for the chicks. It might only have been scavenging scraps of spilt chick food, but I knew that rats were partial to young chicks and were also extremely skilful at dragging them away one at a time to feed their own hungry young. Some years earlier I had seen a rat dragging away a well-grown chick, nearly as big as a partridge. There was no suitable place to set a trap or to put down poison, so I would have to shoot it, but the rat being a nocturnal creature that could be done only at night.

The very next night I wedged an electric torch into the fork formed by two branches of a nearby plum tree, setting the beam to shine across the rat's usual path to the brooder – a tell-tale padded track revealed its route. With my gun under my arm, I stepped into the shadows and waited. I did not have long to wait before my quarry appeared within the patch of light shed by the torch and began scurrying across it. One barrel stopped it in its tracks, though the sound of the single shot in the still, frosty air was deafening and reverberated round the quiet hills like a roll of thunder. With the threat to the chicks removed I was able to return indoors, get into my slippers and enjoy the rest of the evening by the fireside with an easier mind.

Jim Alsop, our neighbour, who with his wife had done so much to help us get started with poultry, was always ready to lend a hand to others. Yet he was himself a magnet for bad luck and often seemed to get more than his share.

On one occasion a carthorse dropped dead, a misfortune not

unknown to horse-owners, but for Jim the loss of his horse was not the end of his troubles. He sent for the knacker man who, when he saw that the dead animal was lying in the middle of a spinney, said it would be impossible to get near enough to hitch a tow-rope to it. Jim, about to set off for the village, left the men shaking their heads and thoughtfully stroking their chins. When he returned, the men and their lorry had gone but a wide smear mark on the wet field showed quite clearly that something had been dragged across it during his absence, and he assumed that the knacker men had succeeded in removing the remains of his horse. However, on visiting the spinney the next morning he discovered that the carcase had been skinned and the hide taken away. Digging a hole among those tree roots would have been an almost impossible task. Exactly how Jim got rid of his pile of unwanted horseflesh I never enquired, and he never enlightened me.

On another occasion one of his best milking cows was drowned during a very dry summer. In common with many others, Jim had no water supply other than a well near the back door of the house and a few ponds dotted around the farm. In a dry summer the ponds dried up, and Jim was then obliged to cart water to the farm or drive his stock to the nearest available water every day. Neither method of dealing with the problem was satisfactory, and milk yields were seriously affected, so Jim, feeling fed up and very frustrated, decided to do something about it. He engaged the services of a water-diviner, with the intention of sinking a well should an adequate supply be found. The diviner did his stuff and found water – lots of it, he said, and work on the well began. After reaching a depth of seven or eight feet, work was suspended until the sides could be safely shored up.

Then the weather broke in a series of violent thunderstorms, and the 'well' suddenly filled with water. During one of the storms a cow startled by the thunder and lightning panicked and dashing across the field crashed through the temporary barrier placed round the excavation and dived headlong into the water. At least, that was how Jim accounted for the accident. When he found her, he saw only two hind legs pointing skywards. Getting the cow out without lifting-gear would have been extremely difficult, so the idea was abandoned; instead, it was decided to leave her where she was, in her ready-made grave. Then it was discovered that those legs would not budge, so an axe was brought and they were hacked off and thrown into the water beside the body. Soil, previously dug out, was then put back where it came from, burying the unfortunate cow and putting an end to Jim's well-digging activities.

Two months or more after our return to the cottage we were still puzzling over why it did not seem as cosy as it had before the fire. At first we thought it hadn't dried out properly, but then the penny dropped and the cold truth dawned on us. The roof, originally of thatch, had been covered with corrugated iron. Very little thatch had been removed when the iron was put on, and this, together with the debris on the bedroom ceilings, had served as a very effective loft insulation. With a tiled roof and pulpboard ceilings, the place would never be cosy and snug again. A change in the layout of both floors during restoration probably made things even worse, though the idea had been to give us more space.

Before it was burned down, a short spiral staircase led out of the living-room through a door only a few feet from the fire, allowing warm air to rise to the bedrooms above. During rebuilding, a straight staircase was installed directly opposite the door opening onto the courtyard and, whenever it was open, allowed cold air to rush in.

When I was visiting at an old cottage in Priors Marston recently (1989), I noticed that the stairway, with its own door, led off from the corner of the living-room a few feet from the cooking range and as far as it could possibly be placed from any door leading to the cold, outdoor world; it reminded me immediately of our old cottage before it had been 'improved'. As in our old cottage, small windows prevented unnecessary loss of heat. The builders of those cottages had never been bombarded with slogans about 'energy-saving': they simply used common sense.

12

When morning gilds the skies

In early summer our neighbour, Jim, asked me if I would chop off the spear thistles – or 'pod thistles', as we called them – in a field nearby. The field, overlooked from our front windows and less than twenty yards from the door, was conveniently near home, so I didn't hesitate and took on the job at a wage of 6 pence an hour. Whether Jim really needed my assistance I wasn't sure; I suspected he was trying to be helpful. Annie liked being out of doors, and with the work so near home, she was able to join me. In beautiful weather, we started early in the morning, between five and six o'clock, while the children were still asleep. Wielding those hoes was tiring work but we enjoyed it, and though it gave us a nasty backache, it also gave us a hearty appetite, and we had no qualms about 'clocking' Annie's time spent on the job. If my backache was worth 6 pence an hour, so was hers.

Side by side, while larks sang overhead, we worked slowly up and down the field. Chiff-chaff and willow warbler were still in full song, and pigeons crooned all around us. These were all content with the world as they found it, fulfilling their lives in their natural environment, and so, I'm sure, were we – a man and a woman working together in the fields, our children safely asleep close by. Thousands of young men and women who would enjoy, and profit from, such a way of life will never have the opportunity of doing so.

My Uncle Jack, the carrier, rented two fields adjoining our

holding, the boundary fence passing less than ten feet from the kitchen window. This good gentleman also found me numerous odd jobs to do and was genuinely glad of my help foddering cattle on the days he was away on his carrying business. Then, one day in the summer of 1939, he surprised us when he said he intended giving up the tenancy of the fields and that if we were interested he would put in a word on our behalf with the landlord. We were more than interested – it was an opportunity we could not afford to miss. The land, twenty acres of it, was glebe belonging to the vicar of Moreton Pinkney, a village about eight or nine miles away, somewhere in the backwoods of Northamptonshire. I had heard of the place, though I hadn't the faintest idea where it was.

One mellow September morning I set off on my bike and was soon bowling along unfamiliar roads. I decided to check that I was on the right course, but the road was completely deserted and there wasn't a house in sight. Then I noticed a man ploughing. He was coming slowly towards the roadside hedge, and when he slewed his plough to run along the headland I shouted to him. He assured me that I would soon come to a signpost and that, in fact, neither the village nor the vicarage was difficult to find.

The vicar, a short, round-faced man with a twinkle in his eye, insisted on showing me his beautiful little church before he would talk business. Half a dozen ladies, up to their ears in flowers and vegetable marrows, were busily engaged in beautifying the building for their Harvest Festival, while a number of other people, including some children, were carrying even more stuff into the church. Apparently satisfied that everything was going well, Mr Martin took me across to the vicarage. He asked a few pertinent questions and said he had received a good report of me from the outgoing tenant. He explained that the rent would remain at £24 per annum for the twenty acres, but nothing was said about maintenance of fences or the selling-off of crops. No agreement was produced, nothing was signed – it was all very friendly and informal, though not very business-like. I rode home feeling a foot taller than when I rode out – I was now tenant in my own right of twenty acres of land.

The twenty extra acres would enable us to increase our stock numbers and, in time, to become less dependent on poultry. Another daylight fox-raid had reminded us that free-range poultry-keeping was an extremely risky business.

We had returned home one beautiful summer afternoon to discover once again the amount of damage a fox can cause among a flock of helpless hens. Dead birds lay scattered over the field; many were badly injured; a few, with feathers torn from their backs, had deep wounds from which blood was still oozing – a deep, savage bite had probably punctured a lung. It was no sight for the squeamish, but we could not turn our backs on it. We had to clear the battlefield, and we began by putting an end to the sufferings of the badly injured – a heart-breaking task for anyone. Only then did we feel free to begin calculating the financial loss inflicted on us, including probable loss of income from eggs for months to come.

Nor were free-range poultry immune to disease. We had thirty lovely Buff Rock pullets which we proudly showed off to all our visitors. Then one began to scour, (diarrhoea), and died within a few days. All were dead in less than a month. We had noticed some nasty droppings under a tree not far from the fowl-house and suspected a diseased wild bird of infecting our poultry with the deadly sickness. The thought crossed our minds that had they been housed indoors we might not have lost a single bird. So much for 'healthy' free-range poultry! The loss of those pullets convinced us that free-range poultry-keeping was not the ideal way of making a living.

The Revd John Woodman was rarely seen wearing anything but his black clerical suit and shovel hat, but he was not an austere man. The vicarage was about a hundred yards from the church, and as I passed it on my way home I often walked along with him, wishing him 'Good night' at the vicarage gate before heading into the fields. He enjoyed a chat, and one Sunday evening (he must have been reading the *News of the World*) he mentioned a well-known film actress who had just married for the umpteenth time. 'That's America,' he said. 'It's like a poultry run.' He was deeply interested in church history, particularly British church history, and he lent me a book on the subject, all about those fine old Celtic saints.

One summer he took the choir on an outing to Regent's Park zoo and to see St Paul's Cathedral. The local carrier, who now ran a small bus, took us to the station at Woodford Halse where we caught an express to Marylebone. On our way back to the station the vicar left us outside a large store, enjoining us not to move, while he popped in to make a purchase. We waited, but no vicar emerged, and time was getting short. One of the ladies suddenly became quite excited and, pointing to a bus, exclaimed, 'That's going to the station.' At that moment it was travelling at walking pace in heavy traffic, and when one of the party shouted, 'Come on!' we all with one accord dashed into the street and scrambled aboard, ignoring the angry conductor's protests and threats.

At the station entrance, the vicar, pacing up and down with his hat in his hand and mopping his forehead, was in quite a state. The silly old man had entered the shop by one door and left by another. But we caught the train with a minute to spare, so all ended well. The last part of my journey was across familiar fields, strangely and restfully quiet after the ceaseless roar of that great city.

Our 1939 harvest began during that memorable first week in September. A few days after the dramatic and sombre announcement that we were 'at war with Germany', we began cutting a track round the wheat with fagging-hooks so that the tractor and binder could get round without fouling the hedge or damaging the standing corn. Seed-time and harvest, knowing nothing of war, would continue as they had from the beginning, though the harvest would now be much more important – and more valuable – than it had been for years.

It was a perfect September morning, the sun slowly dispersing early mist and pigeons murmuring, 'Take two swaths, Percy, take two swaths.' Dad came into the field later with two little boys – somewhere between eight and ten years old, I would have guessed, and each had a cardboard box slung over his shoulder. They showed no interest in what was going on, nor did they throw off their jackets and romp around, and Dad said they had stubbornly refused to leave their gas-masks behind. They said they'd been told they mustn't go anywhere without them. They certainly looked lost and bewildered that first day, but who could blame them? They soon settled down with my parents in the village, but as weeks passed and no bombs fell, those young evacuees, like many others, returned to their city home.

Whenever corn-cutting was in progress, we could expect to be joined by 'Corker', as he was known in those parts. He was a very popular 'rep' for a firm of corn merchants based in Banbury and was on good terms with most of the farmers in his area, some of whom were his customers. In his spare time 'Corker' walked over hundreds of acres of land, a gun under his arm, his spaniel 'nosing' the ground a few yards ahead of him, and a capacious game bag slung at his back. The bag never appeared to have much in it, and filling it was probably not the main purpose of his country rambles – the open air, the companionship of his dog, and a chat with anyone with time to lean over a gate apparently provided the pleasure he sought in his wanderings off the beaten track.

It was uncanny, though, how at harvest-time he would turn up at a farm when only an acre or so of corn remained to be cut, when the game was expected to break cover at any moment. But Corker was always ready to mix business with pleasure, and after rubbing out an ear in the palm of his hand, blowing off the chaff and testing a few grains between his teeth, he would say that he'd like to see a sample after the crop had been threshed. The afternoon he came to watch us cut our wheat proved to be an unusually interesting one.

Corker and the man on the binder were both good shots, so few rabbits were likely to escape once they had allowed themselves to become marooned in an island of corn which shrank by the minute. The island continued to shrink, but not a single rabbit, or hare or bird emerged. We couldn't understand it – it was most unusual. Then, quite unexpectedly, a fox slipped out and began streaking across the stubble, but the hedge was now quite a distance away, and a single shot from one of the guns knocked it over before it had covered half the distance. A few minutes later a second fox broke cover, and then a third, and by the time cutting was finished six foxes had been accounted for, and the mystery of the missing game solved.

We examined the carcases and came to the conclusion that

they were those of a vixen and her litter of fully grown cubs. Had the mother taken her offspring into the field where the poultry were ranging for a lesson in hunting for themselves, they would have had the time of their lives, but the poultry would certainly have suffered terror, death and cruel mutilation once again. Alive, those foxes were a menace; dead, they were harmless as doves.

During the long winter months, time dragged heavily. Friends lent me all the readable books they possessed, but I grew more and more restless with nothing to do, so I looked out an old exercise book and began writing again. I tried keeping a diary, but that soon struck me as a pointless waste of time, and though we could ill afford the money, I once again enrolled with a correspondence college – this time for a course in English and freelance writing.

The work was fascinating and absorbing, but I could see a long, tough haul ahead. However, after a few months steady work I succeeded in selling an article to *Empire Review*, published by Macmillan & Co, for which I received one guinea. Having my first work published by that illustrious house did me no good at all. It carried me into the clouds, and not until the rejection slips began arriving again did I come down to earth, though I did sell an article to *Country Life*, also for one guinea.

Time dragged on winter evenings; on summer evenings there wasn't enough of it; and in haymaking time I found myself engaged in a tug-of-war between the farm and the church. Leaving the hayfield on a summer evening to attend choir practice was always difficult. I felt that I was neglecting my job and leaving others to do the hard work. With great reluctance I gave up my post as organist and stayed away from church lest I allowed myself to be 'talked into it' again.

Then came news that Mr Woodman was seriously ill in hospital. Mrs Woodman, who was acting as temporary organist, came to the farm one day and asked me to go back to the organ for a week or two because she wanted to be with her husband. Though it almost tore me in two, I summoned up from somewhere the callous courage to refuse her request. A few days later I received a letter from the vicar, who was in

St Luke's Hospital, London – he said he hoped I would go back to the organ for a few weeks. Then came one from his wife, who said she was with her husband in London and was hoping to go with him to one of the south-coast resorts where he was to spend a fortnight for rest and convalescence, and would I take the organ for that short time? Before I could reply to those two earnest pleas, we learned that, following an unexpected relapse, the Revd J.H. Woodman had died.

I was quite upset and told myself I had behaved badly. I could not bring myself to go to church, where I might be confronted by the unfortunate widow, but my absence did not cause the church to fall down. Mrs Woodman left the village, the churchwardens found an organist, and church life went on as before. It always does.

At the end of 1939 we were able to draw up a balance sheet of sorts for our poultry-keeping business. Eggs were still making between 1s. 6d. and 2 shillings a dozen; corn for feeding the poultry cost 5 shillings a hundredweight, and meal 7s. 6d. Our crude bookmaking showed that we had made a profit over food costs of £70. That might seem a meagre reward for all the work involved, but when we compared it with the farm worker's wage of 30 shillings for a full week's work, we didn't think it was too bad. We made over £100 the following year, but that was our last in the egg-producing business before war-time restrictions closed us down. We still produced sufficient eggs for our own needs, and we had milk, butter and bacon. These basic foods, taken for granted on most farms and easily obtainable by everyone in peace time, were soon to become extremely scarce and dear. Poultry meat and eggs became luxuries, and poultry food was severely rationed, though there was a brisk trade on the black market. By keeping a few hens in the backyard, many households were able to convert kitchen waste and table scraps into meat and eggs.

Friends and relations from town now seemed able to find the time to visit us more frequently than they had before the war, and the fields were no longer an obstacle. You could see them almost drooling at the mouth as they feasted meat-hungry eyes on the hams and flitches of bacon adorning our sitting-room walls. That it was unhygienic to hang uncooked meat in a warm living-room for several months didn't appear to worry them. Needless to say, none left empty-handed. A chunk cut from a ham, a fat chicken, a dozen eggs or one of Annie's special pork pies made a most acceptable Christmas present. With a plump chicken or a piece of ham, any one of them could have been bribed to rob a bank.

In January 1940 snow began to fall, and it continued to fall steadily until the cottage was almost encircled by snow-drifts three to four feet deep and in places whirled into fantastic shapes by the strong wind. Many gates, stiles and hedges were buried, but I managed to struggle through to the village, greatly relieved to find that we were not completely cut off from the outside world.

Some days later the water running into the yard (our usual supply during the winter) slowed to a trickle, and finally it ceased altogether as frost bit deeper into the ground. For the children's safety and our peace of mind, a permanent cap had been put on the well, but unfortunately the semi-rotary pump we used for raising the water had been burst by the frost. The only water now within reach was in a pond about a hundred yards from the house, but it could be reached only by digging a trench through the deepest snow drifts. That done, I took an axe and chopped a hole through ice a foot thick in the centre of the pond. The first bucket of water I drew out looked as clear as crystal to my eye, though through a microscope it might have looked more like a well-stocked aquarium. However, when it had been strained through a piece of muslin and boiled, we reckoned it was safe to drink. It certainly made a good cup of tea.

The cattle and poultry, all indoors, also needed water, and I was sometimes carrying it in my two buckets until after nine o'clock in the evening. Cattle on a diet of dry, dusty hay are thirsty creatures; fortunately we had no heavy milkers or I would have been hauling water till daybreak.

The weather was bitterly cold, the temperature well below freezing, but strenuous exercise in the clear air was invigorating and pleasant. Bright, twinkling stars almost danced against the dark night sky, and the loudest sound to reach my ears was the 'crunch, crunch' of my boots in the crisp, frozen snow, though from time to time an explosion like the crack of a rifle shot came from a nearby tree, sounding as though some invisible woodsman were trying to split it from top to bottom. Very occasionally the voice of a dog fox shattered the stillness as he barked his way across snow-covered, frost-bound fields. The sound of a dog fox in quest of a mate was a sign that, though we were in the grip of winter, spring was not too far away.

Snow and ice and all the rigours of winter were but entries in a diary when, at six o'clock one mid-April morning, I went out to check the sheep and lambs. Elm trees and hawthorn hedges were displaying beautiful fresh green leaves, and with spring filling the air I half-expected to hear my first cuckoo, but I was disappointed on that particular morning.

The sheep and lambs had been taken from the home field – the nursery – to a field of fresh pasture a little further from home. The pasture was not too rich and lush. Ewes with twins would produce sufficient milk for their offspring, but there was a danger that those with a single lamb would produce more than enough. Too much milk can cause all sorts of trouble – hence my early morning walk to check that all was well.

The sheep had already risen from their night's rest and had suckled their lambs. Now, widely scattered, they were busy grazing, and many of the lambs were also picking at the young grass. Then I noticed a lamb lying by itself near the hedge, where it had probably spent the night. Though it looked bright enough, I was a little concerned. I never liked to see an animal lying by itself, as it was often an indication that something was wrong. As I was about to walk across and put it to its feet and while I was still twenty-five or thirty yards away, I spotted a fox coming across the field. Almost instinctively, I froze and waited to see what the fox would do. As it trotted between the grazing sheep, one or two raised inquisitive heads and watched it for a moment before returning to the business in hand. Once clear of the sheep, it immediately caught sight of the lamb lying on its own and, changing direction slightly, headed towards it. At a distance of four or five feet it halted, studied it intently for what seemed an awfully long time and then began to walk slowly towards the unsuspecting lamb. I stood ready to let out a yell should the fox attack the lamb. It approached to within a foot and held out its nose, as if it were smelling it, while the lamb, equally curious, held up its head; from the slight start each gave, I was sure that their noses had actually touched, though neither seemed unduly alarmed. The fox, its curiosity obviously satisfied, turned and trotted away and was soon out of sight. Nor had it been aware of my presence so near at hand. The lamb, quite unperturbed, still lay with its feet tucked under its body, but when I approached, it leapt to its feet, stretched itself and dashed off across the field to its mother. A young, weakly lamb so near a fox's jaws would have met a very different fate.

If you are a quiet mover, early morning is the time when fox cubs may sometimes be seen at play. A litter of cubs playing and gambolling outside their earth at dawn in early summer makes a truly captivating picture, and they make the perfect subject for any photographer or artist lucky enough to come across these 'delightful' creatures amusing themselves. There is something quite disarming about them; no one can resist them. 'What sweet little creatures,' people say. Beautiful they are, but only as wild animals and in their own environment. Mawkish sentimentality is misplaced – they are wild animals, not near relations of 'Basil Brush' or any other amusing puppet.

13

In a country churchyard

We were busy haymaking one day when we spotted a man with an official-looking folder under his arm heading across the field in our direction. We recognized him as a local farmer, a neighbour almost, who farmed one of the larger farms in the parish. He came up to me, shook me warmly by the hand and complimented me on my excellent crop of hay – it was obvious that his business was with me, and he soon got down to it.

He informed me that the 'War Ag.'* had appointed a panel of farmers to find land suitable for ploughing and cropping with cereals and that, as a member of the panel, he had been allotted the task in our area. He hastened to explain that a farmer from outside the area had already inspected his farm and had scheduled several fields as suitable for corn-growing, and added that, as a grass farmer himself, he was far from pleased, but there was a war on, and it had to be done. He then produced a map and after studying it for a moment said, quite pleasantly, 'You'd better plough this one, Ray – the one we're standing in. It's a smallish field, and it looks fairly level.' Although he had been tactful about it, he had, in fact, served on me a compulsory order to plough and crop the field for the following year's harvest.

---

* The government had appointed War Agricultural Executive Committees throughout the United Kingdom at the beginning of the war. Though soon known by the initials WAEC, a committee was more familiarly known as the 'War Ag'.

My father received an order to plough the rest of the field in which there had been some arable since he and his father had broken the turf with digging-forks. This he had expected to do, as in 1916 – 17, but he was taken aback when he was told he must also plough the adjoining sixteen-acre field. 'Tumble-down' arable when his father took it over, it was now good, sound pasture. He was a great believer in the value of basic slag, and Dad's pastures had repaid his faith in it.

It was not difficult to calculate that our joint arable acreage was about to leap from six acres to thirty. To us, simple, pastoral peasants that we were, the prospect of wrestling with so much heavy clay was quite frightening, and we did not need to be told that any increase in arable would mean a corresponding decrease in available pasture – our plans for keeping more livestock had been knocked on the head; indeed, Dad said that, with two fields under the plough, he would have to sell off his small flock of breeding sheep.

Like most farmers in the area we were ill-equipped for breaking and cultivating heavy clay pasture, but the government had been getting prepared. The War Ag. had a pool of men and a wide range of machinery ready to carry out work anywhere in the county, and these machines were soon busy transforming the face of the Warwickshire countryside. A crawler tractor and a giant plough turned up to plough my field and made short, easy work of it. After a few weeks 'weathering' and, for once, the right amount of rain, it came down to a reasonably good tilth into which we drilled a crop of winter wheat.

Those first wartime crops yielded well, and farmers were able to cash in on fertility stored up in the soil over many years, but deep ploughing had brought to the surface long-dormant seeds of wild oat and charlock, both extremely pernicious weeds; these too flourished in the fertile soil and almost choked succeeding corn crops; in some areas beastly little orange-coloured wire-worms nibbled away at the crop just beneath the surface of the soil, seriously affecting yields. As yet, chemical warfare against pests and crop diseases was in its infancy; nevertheless, farmers succeeded in feeding the British people.

When our oldest child started school, he faced a long, tiring walk across the fields to Priors Marston, but after the first few days he set off cheerfully enough on his own, though for much of the way he was out of sight or earshot of any human habitation. Of the beasts of the field he had no fear. Flocks of sheep grazed in some of the fields he crossed, in others full-grown bullocks followed his progress with mild, slightly curious eyes, yet we were never concerned for his safety, nor afraid he might be molested or knocked down by a speeding car.

In order to make the most of daylight hours during the war the clocks were put two hours ahead of Greenwich Mean Time (GMT) during the summer but were put back only one hour in the autumn, giving us summer-time hours through the winter, with sunrise in December around 9 a.m. This made setting off for school in the morning much less pleasant for the lad during the winter, and made life more difficult for others too.

The pig-killer arrived on the stroke of eight, as arranged, one dark winter morning, and we worked by the light of a smoky hurricane lantern until the straw spread on the carcase was burning well, when we suddenly became two spectral figures moving round the blood-stained victim in the flickering light of the leaping flames like fiends from a Dickens graveyard scene. Black-out regulations had by now accustomed people to working outdoors, however poor the light. Both young and old in this neck of the woods were delighted when war-time tinkering with the clocks came to an end.

Keenly interested in all farm animals since babyhood, my son Reg was particularly fascinated by milking cows, and before he was five years old he began pestering me to let him try his hand at milking. I let him begin on Dumpy, an oldish, docile, easy milker, and sitting on a three-legged stool, with his head tucked into her flank, he looked a 'natural' – in fact, he became quite a competent milker before he started school. His decision to become a cow-keeper was an instinctive one, made very early in life, and the attributes required for the job seemed to have been born with him.

In the summer of 1940 we were producing more milk than

we could carry to Napton in buckets, so there began a daily trip with the horse and float, with a churn containing five or six gallons of milk. For a while we continued to take a case or two of eggs, but the country now needed milk – a valuable, nutritious food, and cows were much less dependent on imported foodstuffs than poultry. At intervals over the next twelve months we bought three cows; the first cost £35, the second £40 and the third £43.

Though one door was closing to us, another was opening: about this time we signed a contract with the Milk Marketing Board and began selling our milk direct to the board under our own label. Our first month's milk cheque, for £12. 0s. 1d. gave us a great thrill. The second was for the staggering sum of £17. 4s. 2d. But before all this could happen, it was necessary to be registered as a milk-producer with the local council. Following my application I was visited by the sanitary inspector, who, after a cursory inspection, suggested that the wooden walls and partitions be well scrubbed down and given a coat of lime-wash and that the brick floors be cleared of their one-inch covering of padded dung and mud, and well washed. He seemed not to notice that we had no piped water and no facilities for cooling the milk, nor did he say a word about drains, probably because he could see for himself that no such refinements existed. Nor did the inspector ever return to satisfy himself that the work had been completed and the buildings brought up to the required standard. Nevertheless, we received a certificate stating that we were duly registered as wholesale producers of milk.

Farmers and farm workers were now busy seven long days a week. Sunday was no longer a day for either rest or worship, and for many, attendance at church or chapel went by the board. I hadn't been inside a church for months, but had I suddenly decided to return, the seven-day week would have made attendance almost impossible. For the moment, growing food to feed the people seemed more important than singing hymns and psalms. Then, quite unexpectedly, I was called back to serve the church at Napton where Dad was still churchwarden.

He told me that the vicar had been trying for ages to fill the vacant post of parish clerk and sexton, but without success, and went on to say that he had 'volunteered' on my behalf, saying I would take the job. I was informed that the duties were light, averaging fewer than a dozen funerals a year. Dad also pointed out that the duties would fit in quite well with my farm work. The suggestion took my breath away for a moment and sent a cold shiver down my spine – I'd never imagined myself as a grave-digger, but I knew there was no wriggling out of it when I was reminded once again that, 'There's a war on, you know.'

My sexton's duties were not too demanding, though difficulties sometimes arose when hay or corn harvest were in full swing and every hand was needed in the field. Whenever it happened that a grave needed to be dug at a busy time, I would set off for the churchyard, a mile and a half distant, very early in the morning, between four and five o'clock, my boots sweeping the dew from the grass as I crossed the fields, while cocks crowed lustily from farmyards and larks sang overhead. I had no watch, and there was no clock on the church tower, so with my sandwiches and bottle of lemonade in my knapsack I carried an alarm clock which, placed in a convenient spot, told me when it was time to put away my pick and spade and re-cross the fields for more heavy work in the hayfield.

It had long been the custom in the parish to toll the 'passing-bell' for an hour immediately after a death, in such a way that the parishioners would know the age and sex of the deceased. After tolling the bell slowly for a minute or so to announce that a death had occurred the ringer would pause. He would then use a kind of morse code. Three strokes of the bell, a pause, three more strokes, another pause, and finally, three more strokes indicated a man's death. Three sets of two strokes, six in all, indicated a woman, and three well-spaced single strokes, a child. He would then toll the necessary number of strokes to indicate the age of the departed, after which he would continue to toll at intervals of one minute, and for about an hour in all, while parishioners were now able to comment, 'So old Tommy Baker's gone at last,' or 'I wonder who they're tolling for, sounds as if it might be a youngster.' Then, on the day of the funeral and about an hour before it was due to take place, a bell known as the 'call bell' was rung for a minute or so, its purpose being to summon from the fields those workers who were to act as bearers; since some might be at a distance, an hour allowed them time to get home, clean up, don their shiny black suits and bowler hats and report for duty. The 'funeral bell' was tolled at intervals of about half a minute from the time the coffin left the house, as near as could be guessed, until it reached the churchyard gate. Immediately after the funeral, a few pulls on the bell-rope announced that all was over and that blinds and curtains could be drawn back.

After the bells were silenced during the war, this ancient ritual of indicating to parishioners by means of the bells the sequence of events connected with the death and burial of a resident came to an end; it was never revived.

Though I have no idea how many graves I dug, I do recall quite vividly some incidents associated with a few of them. For instance, I remember Hugh, probably in his late seventies, coming to watch me make a start at his late wife's grave. I assumed he had come to make sure I was digging at the right place – the spot he and his wife had reserved for their common grave, but he made no comment as I marked out the grave and began digging. It was most unusual for a bereaved person to look on while a loved-one's grave was being dug, and I didn't quite know what to make of Hugh. He appeared to be well satisfied with what he saw and stood looking on with hardly a word spoken until I began to feel quite uncomfortable under his steady gaze. I was wishing he would go away and leave me to get on with the job when he suddenly asked me, somewhat brusquely, to let him take a turn with the spade. It was an unexpected and quite surprising request, but I could see that he was in earnest, so I stepped out of the shallow grave and handed over the spade.

Hugh took off his jacket, slithered clumsily down into the grave and worked steadily while I sat and rested nearby. After about a quarter of an hour he clambered out and put down the spade. He mopped his face and large bald head on a red spotted handkerchief, picked up his jacket and walked away. Tight-lipped, he tried to hide his emotion, but glistening eyes betrayed him. It was obvious that his only reason for coming to the churchyard had been to render his beloved companion the last service he could possibly render her on this earth, and he had done it.

Almost as poignant is my recollection of an old lady's funeral. Her Christian name was Sally; her surname I do not remember. Sally had been taken to an institution of some kind after the doctor had decided that she was no longer capable of looking after herself. She had no family and no money, so, though she was a native of the parish, they gave her a pauper's funeral. There were no mourners, and no flowers; the only people present were the vicar, the undertaker and his men, me (sexton) and one onlooker, a woman who lived close by and had been watching the proceedings from the churchyard fence. It was a brief, brisk affair, and very little time was wasted.

I did my job of filling in the grave as conscientiously as possible; but without a single flower, tidy though it was, that grave proclaimed 'pauper' to all who passed by. Then, as I was patting the last piece of turf into place with the back of my spade, the woman – who, I thought, had been looking on out of idle curiosity – came into the churchyard with a bunch of freshly gathered flowers in her hand. After placing her flowers carefully on the grave, she stood in respectful silence for a moment and then explained that they were from her own garden and that on several previous occasions she had placed flowers on a pauper's grave. 'I'm sure they'd like to know someone had remembered,' she said.

The birth of a baby at Bethlehem was being celebrated in the village with all the usual festivities when I was called to dig a grave for an infant only a few weeks old when it died. The weather was bitterly cold, and the ground was frozen rock-hard. The day of the funeral was cold, the leaden-grey sky full of snow. During the short service an occasional snow-flake drifted slowly down, alighting softly and silently on the small, white casket the father was holding in his arms.

Pale and grim-faced when it was all over, he had some difficulty in dragging the weeping mother away from her baby. When they were gone, I did my best to fill in the little grave, leaving the frozen clods piled on top to await a thaw. Large, feathery flakes of snow began to fall before I had finished, and when I finally left, the churchyard lay under a cold, white pall.

Some years later I chanced to be in the churchyard around Easter-time. The sun was shining and the clouds were high – billowy, white clouds drifting slowly across a blue sky. Recalling that baby's funeral in very different weather, I looked around for the grave but failed to find it. There was no memorial stone, no mound, not even a jamjar to mark the spot. Instead, I saw a level piece of turf, with old, dead grass and young green grass growing through it, all covered with a carpet of pale yellow primroses.

We felt we were getting more involved in the war when a searchlight unit was set up in a roadside field we crossed on our way to Napton. One day I called at the cookhouse and left some eggs. The men seemed delighted with them, so I took to calling about once a week and soon got to know some of the men quite well. Three of them turned up at our door one afternoon and had brought with them a few things they thought we would appreciate – a large carton containing a few pounds of cornflakes and some dried beans. The cornflakes were little better than the flaked maize we fed to the stock before the war, and the beans, soaked for hours and hours, were still as hard as bullets, so we tossed them into the pig-swill.

Then these young men in uniform began coming to the farm in the evenings, finding their way across the fields in the darkness. They enjoyed a chat round the fire, and a cup of coffee or cocoa before they left, but never stayed later than ten o'clock. We kept our wits about us, fearing they might be 'on the scrounge', but we needn't have worried. What we gave them they accepted graciously, and anything they asked for they paid for before they left. They obviously missed their own homes and appreciated the 'homeliness' of our sitting-room and fireside as a welcome alternative to their quarters – cold, wooden huts. Some members of the unit made friends in Napton, while others preferred the companionship of the public houses in their off-duty hours.

As time passed, it became clear that our friends on the searchlight were engaged in activities more serious than drill.

Air raids on Midland cities had begun, and we heard the drone of planes and the sound of air-raid sirens almost every evening, and saw searchlights scanning the sky, but so accustomed did we become to these goings-on that we hardly noticed them.

However, one evening in November 1940 the unmistakable throb of planes passing overhead at a considerable altitude seemed as though it would never cease, and the sound of what we assumed was anti-aircraft fire was more noticeable and much more persistent than usual. Occasionally the thud and explosion of bombs being jettisoned or released short of their target shook the house. Somewhat alarmed at the unusual commotion, we went outside, curious to learn the cause of it all. Searchlights were sweeping the sky in every direction; there was the sound of anti-aircraft fire and the shuddering crunch of bombs, while to the north of us the sky looked as though it were on fire. We stood and watched, aghast yet fascinated, until we were stiff with cold. Next morning we learned that we had been watching the destruction of Coventry on 14 November 1940, although few details came through until later in the day.

The great exodus also began that day. Many residents of the stricken city who had stubbornly 'stayed put' through all previous bombing raids now decided that enough was enough, and set out determined to find sanctuary for their children. Cars explored villages and remote hamlets, bumped along narrow lanes and gingerly nosed their way down rutted farm tracks at the risk of getting stuck in the mud.

Marooned as we were in muddy fields, no cars were able to reach us, but a woman in the village, who knew us quite well, asked if we would take two boys, aged five and seven. Though not reluctant to help, we pointed out how remote and isolated we were, and that parents would find considerable difficulty in visiting their children during the winter; we also pointed out that our cottage was very small, with limited sleeping-accommodation. But such drawbacks counted for nothing with the doughty volunteer who had undertaken to find homes for as many children as possible, and so Annie agreed to take in the two boys.

At the weekend a couple, the woman in a three-quarter-length fur coat, arrived at the door with two boys. After a cup of tea we showed them the primitive accommodation we had to offer, and from a few asides by the mother, who wasn't the least bit afraid of the sound of her own voice, we gathered that her boys had been used to a home much better than we were offering them. Nevertheless, she seemed as anxious as her husband that they should be left with us. It was almost dark when the couple tore themselves away from their tearful offspring. The two little boys now entrusted to our care turned a household of five into one of seven.

Both boys settled down well after the day or two needed to get over the shock of being separated from their parents. The older one, Tony, shouldered his satchel and gas mask and walked across the fields with Reg to school at Priors Marston. With the addition of evacuated children, the school was full to bursting, and the staff had been augmented with teachers from the city's depleted schools.

The boys' parents came to the farm regularly every weekend. Leaving the car at the roadside, they gallantly tackled the muddy fields on foot in the foulest weather. Mother always bade the boys a tearful, smothering farewell, the younger one, John, obviously expecting to be taken home on each occasion. But almost before the parents were out of sight, the boys would resume their play, and they always came to the table for their next meal with unimpaired appetites.

Though our young evacuees never showed any interest in the farm animals, they did like exploring the fields with our own children and were quite thrilled when they were shown a moorhen's nest with eggs in it, and during the one summer they spent with us they thoroughly enjoyed playing in the hayfield. Their father sometimes brought a camera with him, and we have a snapshot of all the children sitting together in front of a half-built haystack.

However, as soon as the worst of the bombing appeared to be over, their mother, naturally anxious to have her children at home with her, carted them off to the city, and we never heard from them, or of them, again. The big table was put back in its place in the dairy.

Another person who shared our table for a few days, though not our roof, was Jimmy Kelly, an itinerant Irish labourer. A local farmer allowed Jimmy to occupy a small brick shed near some outlying farm buildings. The shed boasted an open hearth and a chimney, enabling him to make himself tolerably comfortable without endangering barn or stacks with his fire. One cold January day I found Jimmy trying to do some hedge-cutting. Snow had fallen a few weeks earlier but had now begun to thaw. Ditches were full of water and melting snow, and drifted snow still covered the base of the hedges. Jimmy was trying to light a fire with a few damp sticks and a piece of paper, in the open air, against a cold north-west wind, in the hope that it would at least warm his knees while he ate his bite of food.

Annie made me bring him into the house so that he could eat in comfort. She also supplied him with a good helping of hot food, for which he seemed genuinely grateful, and for the few days he was working near us he shared our fireside and our midday meal.

Some people might have described our cottage as a hovel, and our food as subsistence food, lacking variety; Jimmy Kelly, eyeing the bacon hanging on the walls of our cosy sitting-room, might have said we lived in a palace and that we fared sumptuously every day.

14

The hunt is up

One day in early January 1941 I was battling my way across the fields on my way to the village in the face of a strong north wind and walking, whenever possible, in the shelter of the hedge, when, chancing to raise my eyes for a moment as I passed under an old elm tree, I found myself looking into a pair of keen, steady eyes. Twenty feet above the ground, a fox lay, crouched along a limb and as motionless as a statue. Though startled on seeing it, I made no sudden movement. I wanted the fox to think I hadn't spotted it, so I lowered my eyes slowly and continued walking at the same steady pace until I was well beyond the tree; then, making a wide detour, I hurried home for my gun. On my return I found the fox in exactly the same position, but the moment I hesitated in my step and began to raise the gun, that statue sprang to life and disappeared into a hole in the tree.

In an adjoining field my neighbour and his man were foddering cattle, but they did not need much persuading to leave their work and return with me to investigate the tree. The top had been blown off years before, and there were holes in the trunk where large limbs had been broken off by strong winds. One man took my gun and began climbing the tree, which leaned precariously over a pond covered with ice some two or three inches thick. Ten feet up he came to the first hole and peeped into it. To his astonishment, he found himself almost rubbing noses with a fox. Oblivious of any possible danger, he pushed the barrel of the gun into the hole

131

and pulled the trigger; a moment later he threw a dead fox to the ground. Six feet higher was the hole into which I had seen a fox disappear. It was still there, and after a shot had been discharged into the hole a second dead fox was thrown down.

Without its top, the upper end of the trunk looked like a chimney-pot, its top edge broken and jagged. When my friend peered down the 'chimney', he was sure he could make out yet another fox, and with his last cartridge he fired into the hole. He reached down and found the fox, quite dead, but crouching behind it was its companion, snarling and very much alive. This fourth fox was eventually dragged from its lair with a looped cord. It fell to the ground and, finding itself uninjured, made a dash for freedom, but Bob, the sheepdog, who had accounted for many a fox in his time, leaped towards it, and after a short, fierce battle he was able to add one more to his tally.

Those foxes had obviously found a comfortable block of flats for their winter quarters, each an independent unit with its own access to a warm, dry bedroom. Hunting folk might brand our action 'unsporting', but little or no hunting was being done, and foxes were becoming too numerous. Those in another camp would say that what we did was cruel and unnecessary, but four adult foxes holed up together during the winter, when they would find food hard to come by, were, we believed, a very real threat to both poultry and new-born lambs. We were simply being practical.

Every year, round about tupping-time, letters appear in the press vociferously decrying fox-hunting, followed by others as ardently defending it. Among farmers there are those who would have it banned tomorrow, and others who enjoy nothing better than a day in the field.

Many farmers are opposed to hunting not because they consider it cruel but because of the behaviour of the folk on horseback. Too many riders to hounds are arrogant, rude, snobbish and completely devoid of courtesy, and show not the least consideration for the farmers over whose land they gallop not as a right but as a privilege. If there are louts in our city streets, there are also louts in pink and black in the hunting field who would love to trample an objecting farmer into the mud if they thought they could get away with it.

A few years ago a solitary hunt-follower who had apparently lost contact with the main body came through a gate into one of my fields and, leaving it wide open, set off across the field at a brisk trot. He then spotted me and, pointing behind him with his crop, bawled out, 'Shut that gate, my man.' My hackles rose, but I succeeded in keeping the lid on my temper while I ordered him, quite civilly, I thought, to return by the way he had come and to shut and fasten the gate behind him. One unbelievable incident involved a young woman whose conduct and manners led us to conclude that, though she might be a woman, she was certainly no lady. That such attitudes still persist in this enlightened twentieth century is quite incredible.

There are farmers who have suffered deep distress as a result of the high-handed conduct of hunting folk, and no one is surprised when the unfortunate victim of these louts declare their land 'out of bounds'. Unfortunately their wishes, instead of being respected, are often callously ignored. An MFH may do his utmost to foster and retain the goodwill of farmers in his territory with courtesy visits at the beginning of the season, asking permission to hunt over their land, and he may promise, in good faith, that the hunt will not trespass on land known to be out of bounds, but a few individuals, wilfully defying all instructions, make a master's life extremely difficult. Broken fences are usually repaired promptly and compensation is paid for other damage caused, but nothing is paid for the privilege of hunting over a farmer's land.

The squirearchy, what is left of it, well-heeled landowners and retired colonels are no longer the only people who can afford to ride to hounds. Show-business people, television celebrities and pop singers now enjoy a day's hunting, and their behaviour in the field is even worse than that of the other lot. They have no country background and no knowledge of farming – fields are a playground, kindly provided for them to gallop over as and when they please. They have no idea of the terrible injuries caused when a herd of cattle is stampeded into a barbed-wire fence, nor of what can happen when a gate is left open and cattle or horses are allowed to stray onto a busy road.

Most letters to the press on the emotive subject of fox-hunting are from readers violently opposed to it. The letters, couched in exaggerated language, are peppered with such absurd words as 'barbaric', 'uncivilized' and 'blood lust'. Most normal people would confess to feeling a certain amount of sympathy for the fox, or any other hunted creature (it is a natural and laudable sentiment), but those who, in their misplaced zeal to save the fox from the jaws of the hounds, clamour for hunting to be stopped have failed to appreciate the probable consequences of a total ban on hunting. There would obviously be a steady rise in the fox population and a corresponding decline in its food-supply, and eventually the general health of the fox would deteriorate, thus rendering it more susceptible to disease. During the last war, when no grouse-shooting took place, numbers increased dramatically, and in his book *One Man's Happiness* Lord Tweedsmuir (John Buchan) relates that dead grouse lay around in thousands one winter, victims of disease and starvation.

To prevent this happening to the fox, an authorized cull might be carried out from time to time, probably by marksmen, but whether old or young, fit or sick would be killed could not be guaranteed. A young, healthy fox could be destroyed while an old animal near the end of its hunting life might escape the cull and the following winter would crawl into a hole to die slowly of starvation.

When a strong, healthy fox is pursued by hounds, it usually succeeds in outrunning or outwitting its pursuers – fit and healthy, it survives to perpetuate its kind, as Nature intends it should. An old, sick or unfit fox gives the hounds a run but is eventually caught and dispatched, leaving more food for the young and for the next generation, as Nature intends it should. Without this harsh law – the survival of the fittest, many wild creatures would have been extinct centuries ago. By the same law, few wild creatures reach a ripe old age.

Much as we may dislike those quaintly dressed folk on horseback, the fact remnains that at present hunting is the most humane, most effective and most natural method of controlling the number of foxes. However, hunting people need to put their house in order. They must treat farmers fairly and courteously, and they must also convince the general public that they no longer tolerate barbarous 'blooding' rites and do not artificially introduce foxes into an area for 'sport's' sake. They must also deal much more strictly with those individuals who behave badly and so give their whole fraternity a bad name.

There are those who now regard hunting as an anachronism which should go the way of the cross-roads gallows and the thumb-screw, but few true-born country folk would share that view. They follow the chase in cars, on bikes and on foot, thrilled by the sound of the horn, the thud of hooves and the baying of hounds; stirred by the overall spectacle of the hunting scene, all hearts beat a little faster. Some make a point of attending the meet simply to admire the horses and, especially, the sleek hounds – a forest of quivering tails. A certain Stratford-upon-Avon man who admired the hounds wrote, 'Their heads are hung with ears that sweep away the morning dew.' The thrill of the chase stirred him to add, 'A cry more tuneable was never hollar'd to, nor cheered by horn.' (*A Midsummer Night's Dream*, Act IV, scene 1.)

At dusk one winter afternoon three weary-looking horses and three mud bespattered riders passed our gate, and I fell to musing about them.

> They go clip-clopping home at the end of the day,
> Their clobber all spattered with mire,
> To a lovely hot bath, a bottle of Scotch
> And a snooze by a crackling fire;
> To dream of the fox they 'lost' on the hill,
> Or the 'meet' next week at 'The Bell',
> While the farmer whose sheep they half-frightened to death
> Is wishing them all into ...

With thirty acres of arable land to harvest, we needed a binder of our own, and succeeded in buying one at a local farm sale. Lots of other farmers were as badly in need of arable implements as we were, and bidding was exceedingly brisk, but it was finally knocked down to us for £45. It was an oldish machine of American make, but it gave us very little trouble.

The only serious breakdown we had occurred on a glorious, sunny afternoon – and, of course, it was a Saturday afternoon. We had been cruising comfortably round a lovely clean crop of wheat, the knife was chattering merrily and sheaves were being tossed out with monotonous regularity to the 'clack, clack' of the ejector when, without the slightest warning, the wooden draw-bar snapped in two. One glance was enough to tell us that this was no wire-and-string job – a new bar was needed, so, rather than allow the binder to stand idle over the weekend in such lovely harvest weather, we decided to have a go at making a draw-bar ourselves, using materials and tools we had to hand, inadequate though they were.

From a nearby hedge we chopped down a likely-looking elm sapling, trimmed it off and carried it to the binder. After measuring and cutting off the correct length, we took the billhook and shaped the ends to fit the castings on the machine. Half a dozen holes were bored, luckily in the right places, to take the bolts, and in less than two hours we were tossing out sheaves again. That rustic, home-made bar, intended to see us over the weekend, was still sound when we finally pensioned off the binder and pushed it into a corner of the rickyard.

The extra acres of corn being grown by almost every farmer kept threshing contractors busy throughout the year, and there were times when they were quite unable to satisfy the heavy demands on their services. But again the War. Ag. came to our help and on one occasion supplied us with a machine and a skilled operator to take charge of it. It was a lightly built, all-metal contraption – American, of course, and originally designed for work on the prairies. Known as a 'peg drum', it was quite unlike the heavy, wooden threshing-drums of native breed.

Dust, chaff, weed seeds and straw, the latter chopped to shreds, were all discharged from a single spout at the side of the machine, leaving us a pile of useless rubbish, unfit for food or bedding and, as we discovered, almost impossible to burn; nor did the peg drum make a satisfactory job of cleaning the corn. North American farmers might have been satisfied with its performance but, though it required a smaller gang of workers than the familiar wooden drum, in our English shires, where straw and chaff were valuable commodities, the machine was not a success. In fact, we never saw one again.

In the summer of 1941 a neighbour, whose small farm adjoined ours, told us he intended giving up the farm (he wasn't prepared to tackle all the ploughing 'they' had ordered him to do), and he thought we might be interested in taking it on. He said he hoped to move into the village but would keep on with his job as postman. The farm of forty-three acres joined our recently acquired glebe fields and extended to the road, the entrance gate being about a mile from Priors Marston village. It offered exciting possibilities. Another wonderful opportunity had turned up at exactly the right moment.

We were shown round the house and were pleased to find it contained four bedrooms. We were thrilled to bits when we noticed the sink in the kitchen with a pump above it – undreamed-of luxury, indeed. Not one to let the grass grow under my feet, I got on my bike and went to see the landlord, a farmer who lived in the village. He was pleased to see me and said he remembered helping to put the corrugated-iron roof on the cottage at the beginning of the 1914 – 18 war, prior to going in the army. Without fuss or cross-examination, I was offered the tenancy of the holding, the rent to remain at £55 per annum for the forty-three acres. Once again, no agreement was signed. We were to take possession in March 1942.

Although we were moving only a short distance, we were quite upset when the time came to leave the house. Just as Mother had in 1916, we left a few odds and ends behind, including curtains at the windows. We hoped that one day we would be able to return to what we had come to regard as our 'real home'. But we had to be practical; our second child was now old enough for school, and we badly needed the extra acres, even though two of the farm's four fields were under an 'order' to be ploughed and cropped for the following year's harvest.

The extra farm work now confronting me, and the greater distance from Napton, obliged me to relinquish the post of parish clerk and sexton. The manual work had been hard – digging a grave had sometimes meant chiselling through a foot of solid rock, a muscle-toning exercise which gave me brawny shoulders and a ravenous appetite.

When I walked away from the churchyard for the last time as

sexton, I realized that I had, in some strange way, enjoyed the work, performing the last but essential rites for residents of my native village. My mother's family, still living in the village, were here when Prince Rupert and his men jogged along the Daventry to Southam road on their way to Edge Hill during the civil war, collecting John Shuckburgh and his tenants as they went.

I once heard a clergyman say that the service for the Burial of the Dead was the most beautiful service in the Prayer Book, and hearing the Revd Francis Aylwin read it many times, I knew exactly what he meant. High on that windy hill, the sleeves of his surplice billowing around him, it was often necessary for him to raise his voice so that all might hear him say, as only he could, 'I heard a voice from heaven saying, Write ... even so saith the Spirit; for they rest from their labours.'

Something more than nostalgia sends people back to their birthplaces to end their days; something more than nostalgia draws people from the other side of the globe to scratch around old gravestones in town cemetery and country churchyard, and to pore over dusty documents in search of clues to their origins. From all over the world they come, bent on building up their family trees and on tracing their roots as far back in time as possible.

Shortly before I gave up my job, an elderly gentleman came to me in the churchyard and, after telling me his name, said he was over from Canada and was enquiring about his family. I was unable to help, so I sent him along to the vicarage, where, presumably, he obtained some information for which he was very grateful, because a few months later a package arrived from Canada containing an anonymous gift of a pair of white silk bookmarks for use in the Bible on the lectern.

When all the 'scheduled' ploughing had been completed, Dad and I had around fifty acres of arable between us, and as harvest time approached, we decided we would need some full-time help, so we each engaged a 'land girl'. Mine turned out to be an unfortunate misfit. When I asked her to milk a cow, she stubbornly refused to touch the cow's teats. 'I can't,' she whimpered. 'I can't.' It was obvious that the thought of

making physical contact with those spongy, fleshy pro-
tuberances was quite repulsive to her. The authorities, always
anxious to see that the girls were happy in their work and that
farmers were supplied with the type of girl they required,
found Mollie a job in a market garden and sent me a
replacement.

Of all the jobs on the farm, threshing was by far the dirtiest
and most exhausting, yet despite the filth neither farmer nor
worker dreamed of wearing a mask or goggles, though
sheaves of unthreshed corn came out of the stack matted
together with moulds of every colour, from white through to
black. When threshing was in progress, workers were
enveloped in a dense cloud of dust which they would inhale
until work finished for the day, when they would emerge
from the gloom, blackened faces showing up the whites of
their eyes. That farmers' lung and other chest troubles were
not more common and that their health was not more
seriously affected must have been due to the stamina and
sound constitution of the men and women, including the
gallant girls of the Women's Land Army, who worked in
those appalling conditions. The modern combine-harvester is
also a marvellous creator of dust but operators usually wear
mask and goggles, and to cut down the ear-shattering noise
ear-muffs are often worn.

Frances, five feet tall and lightly built, coped well with
what must have been unusually heavy work for her, and
proved to be an absolute brick. She was always willing to have
a go at anything, however mucky or unpleasant and whatever
the weather. She and the others spent many a long, weary day
in the harvest field and at the threshing without a grumble;
and on a winter day they would pull swedes or cut kale for
the cattle with ice coating the leaves. We were surprised at
their stamina – most of those city-bred girls were tougher
than they looked. Frances remained with us until we no
longer needed her help, and she exchanged Christmas cards
with us for years afterwards.

Her parents spent a weekend with us one summer. On their
first evening they decided to stroll into the village, a distance
of a little over a mile, to enjoy a quiet pint at one of the pubs,
and they invited me to join them. At the first house, a notice

on the door announced, 'No beer', and a similar card on the second house bore the same sad news. Undaunted, they decided to walk a further mile and a half to the next village and try their luck at the only pub in the place. Fortunately no heart-breaking notice was posted on the door. Leg-weary and thirsty, they found a warm welcome and cool, refreshing beer in the Butchers' Arms. It had been a hot day, and even I was glad of a drink, paid for by my friends, of course. Then we walked home again. All that effort – 2½ miles there and 2½ miles back for a glass of beer.

Before the war large numbers of peewits nested in some of the fields near us. Damp, undrained pastures with clumps of rushes and tussock grass in them abounded in food and provided the birds with suitable nesting-sites. Their diving and wheeling, their loud yet plaintive cry of 'pee-wit' was part of our countryside, but as more and more land was put under the plough their numbers decreased. A large field on an adjoining farm had been a favourite nesting-place for years. After the field came under the plough, successful nesting became impossible, though a few pairs did try. Then came the year when only one pair arrived and began wheeling and diving around the spot they had obviously selected for a nesting-site. Then a tractor and disc harrows went into the field and travelled backwards and forwards across it, breaking the rough clods down into a fine tilth. After the harrowing the birds were still around, but then came the drill to sow the corn and more harrows. The poor birds were forced to admit defeat and left to try elsewhere; and that was the last we saw of peewits trying to breed near us. However, they did not desert us completely: large flocks arrive in the autumn. quiet and subdued in manner, they search the fields for food throughout the winter, accompanied by a host of gulls, and, like the gulls, depart when spring arrives.

Other ground birds also suffer when farm machines are at work. I was mowing off some rough grass in a pasture field one day in late summer when a bird darted away from the front of the cutter bar, and a moment later I caught sight of a clutch of khaki-coloured eggs. They were partridge eggs and were quite warm, but there were also some tell-tale spots of blood on them. These told me that the bird, probably the hen, had stayed on the nest just a moment too long and that I had injured her, probably fatally; but, injured or not, I knew that she would not return to her nest now that the sheltering tuft of grass had gone. I took the eggs home but neither we nor our neighbours had a broody hen available. I then rang the gamekeeper at Shuckburgh Hall, but he wasn't the least bit interested. He said nothing could be done and that if they had been pheasants'eggs it would have made no difference – it was too late, the season was over. With a feeling of regret tinged with a little guilt, I realized tht I had no option but to throw away the eggs and the developing chick they contained.

Ground birds are vulnerable at any age. I was strolling along the hedge-side one morning, my two collies at my heels, when a strong covey of pheasants lumbered into the air from almost under my feet. I was startled by the sudden commotion, but the alert younger dog shot past me like a flash, and though the birds were six or seven yards ahead in no time and at least five feet above the ground, the dog leapt into the air and caught one of the half-grown chicks in his jaw – the quickest and cleanest bit of fielding I'd ever seen. He took his catch through the hedge, out of sight of his companion, but caught up with us five minutes later with a very self-satisfied expression on his face, unless he was preening himself and asking, 'Aren't I a clever dog?'

At catching something for the pot I was unlucky. I did once set a snare and hoped for a rabbit. I visited the snare everyday for some days and then forgot all about it. One winter day, with snow on the ground, I chanced to pass the spot, and there, half-buried under the snow, lay a rabbit. I took it up – we would have rabbit for dinner. Then I discovered it was heavy with young; that put me off rabbit for a while. Then myxomatosis appeared. The sight of rabbits crawling around with bloodshot, bulging eyes and swollen heads put us off rabbit for good. We haven't touched it since, though it had once been an enjoyable dish served up with thick gravy and plenty of onions.

15

For the beauty of the earth

Soon after our arrival at the farm I bought a nice roan Shorthorn heifer, freshly calved, from our landlord for £26 as a start towards expanding the dairy herd, but an exceptionally hot, dry summer halted us in our tracks and taught us that without a reliable water-supply dairy farming was quite impossible. The ponds dried up, compelling us to put all the cattle in the home pasture, where we carried water to them pumped from the well until that also ran dry. Without a drop of water on the farm we were in serious trouble. The lowing of cattle crying for water is a mournful, distressing sound, and one not easily forgotten.

We informed the county executive officer of our plight, and he promised to do what he could to help. Sooner than we expected, a Leamington fire brigade tanker loaded with water pulled into the yard. The water, we suspected, had been taken from the River Leam. We had no storage tanks of any description, so it was poured into the empty well, where we hoped it would not evaporate or leak away. Always gluttons for punishment, we now had to pump the water out of the well by hand into buckets which we carried across the yard and poured into troughs for the cattle to drink. Sometimes it seemed as though they would never stop drinking. For household use we carted four or five gallons from the village twice a week in a milk churn.

We were extremely grateful to Leamington fire brigade, as the fire-fighters were then called, for keeping us supplied with water from the Leam through that long, dry summer; nor did we grumble about the charge made for the service. With temperatures still reaching the eighties in September, we scanned the cloudless sky anxiously every day for sight of a cloud bringing relief to thirsty pastures and thirstier cattle.

Between the wars, cattle-breeding was not taken seriously by many farmers, who, provided they got their cows in calf, were not greatly interested in the sire or his ancestors. If it was a bull and knew what to do and could do it, that was all that mattered to them. Bull licensing, aimed at eliminating the poorly fed, poorly bred 'scrub' bull, was successful to some extent, but unlicensed bulls were kept at outlying buildings, and neighbours would take their cows to them, paying a small fee or no fee at all. Dad kept a registered bull and charged a reasonable fee for its services, but he discovered that a few farmers were taking their cows along without his knowledge and did not come forward with the fee. This mean practice was not only annoying: it risked the health of our cows and the health of the cows of honest neighbours. Contagious abortion was dreaded by every cow-keeper.

The introduction of artificial insemination by the Milk Marketing Board changed all that, and after a few years the quality of livestock began to improve and has continued to do so. The scheme has been of enormous benefit to dairy farmers, helping them to improve milk yields and quality, and farmers generally to take a pride in the appearance and performance of their stock. During the years I used the service, the conception rate was high, and a second visit by the inseminator was seldom necessary.

John Woodman was succeeded by the Revd Mr Cripps as vicar of the parishes of Priors Hardwick and Priors Marston, but beyond shaking hands with him on the rare occasions I attended church I had no other contact with him throughout his short ministry. On Wednesday evenings he held a service of intercession for those on active service, when he read out all their names slowly and distinctly. Congregations, drawn from the two parishes, were good and included a number from each of the three Nonconformist chapels.

When I began attending church again more regularly, an

unmarried man, probably in his early forties, had recently settled in. He had a charming personality, and before I realized what was happening I was on the organ stool again, this time on a purely voluntary basis. On Good Friday I sat on that stool for three solid hours without once moving off it.

John Clementson, despite his charming personality, was forthright and outspoken and was not afraid of 'stirring it'. He had not been with us long before he let it be known that the churchyard was the property of the church and was maintained in good order for the benefit of the whole parish by members of the church – Nonconformists and others who did not contribute towards its upkeep should expect to be buried on the far side of the churchyard, where dead flowers and other rubbish were dumped. This remark caused the expected storm, though some chapel folk agreed that the vicar had a point, and a number of donations were received towards the upkeep of the churchyard. Nevertheless, many church people, as well as chapel, were dismayed at his remarks and said they were 'unchristian'.

Probably because he had two churches to care for, he encouraged me to offer myself as a candidate for the office of reader (lay minister) and arranged for me to see the rural dean, the Revd Canon O.M. Jones, rector of Southam, the same breezy gentleman who had offered to teach me Latin or Greek some years earlier. As ebullient as ever, Canon Jones took me into his large, comfortable study, where we sat and talked awhile; then, before I left, he put his arm round my shoulders and we knelt on the hearthrug and recited together that beautiful old hymn, translated from the Latin by Bishop Cosin, 'Come, Holy Ghost, our souls inspire'. That was a most moving and quite unforgettable experience. A public library now stands on the site once occupied by the rectory.

Once again I was embarked on a course of study and about a year later was helping the vicar by conducting Morning or Evening Prayer most Sundays at one or other of his two churches.

During the winter of 1949 I submitted a couple of paragraphs of 'country notes' to the editor of the *Leamington Spa Courier* and was surprised to see them in print a fortnight later. Those paragraphs were the beginning of a feature which ran, with breaks during the busy summer months, for nearly ten years. On one of my rare visits to the office, Mr Knight, the editor gave me a very instructive and interesting guided tour of the printing works.

Though I was paid 30 shillings for each of my contributions, I could not forget that the farm paid the rent and fed and clothed the family, and I always felt uncomfortable sitting indoors at a desk when there was work to be done in the fields. In fact, most of the real work connected with the writing could be done only out of doors, and it kept me on the alert whatever I was doing. To see for the first time things I hadn't been aware of before was a stimulating experience: the inconspicuous hazel catkins, a first sighting of a yellow wagtail or the glorious apparel of a butterfly. The keener eyes and ears needed to help me find my material probably prevented my senses becoming dulled. The following piece, published in the *Courier* on 1 May 1959, explains how a young countryman experienced, observed and noted the uncertain glory of an April day.

A Lambing Storm

The wind freshens and becomes very noticeably colder. The sun disappears behind a mountainous mass of dark, quickly-moving cloud. In a matter of minutes it is as cold as winter. Rain slants down from the darkened sky and stings the face with its icy needles. A minute later the rain turns to hail, and the young man on the tractor decides to seek shelter under the hedge with a sack pulled round his shoulders. But there is little shelter to be had; the hedge has not yet thickened out with its screen of summer leaves.

Above the noise of the wind and the pattering of the hail, the ploughman hears the plaintive bleat of a new-born lamb, and recalls his father's name for these cold storms. He called them lambing storms.

The headland has now collected muddy puddles, and the whole scene is bitterly cold, bleak and cheerless. But even as he watches the hailstones collecting in little heaps against the dead grass along the hedgeside, the cloud passes over, and the hail stops as suddenly as it began.

A patch of bright blue sky appears overhead and grows rapidly larger, the sun emerges as if by magic, warm and inviting, and a brilliant rainbow arcs the sky.

The hedges are hung with glistening raindrops, while their opening leaves are turned a wonderful shade of green by the bright sunlight. Overhead, the sky is full of lark song. The lambing storm is over.

In the mid 1940s we were able to afford a second-hand car, a 1936 Ford 8, for which we paid £43. Unfortunately the farmhouse stood one field back from the road, and across the field there was no hard track, so, unable to cross during the winter, we left the car at the roadside.

One winter day – in 1952, I think it was – a lorry-driver dumped a load of basic slag, several tons of it, at the roadside because he was afraid to venture across the field with his vehicle. As a result, I was obliged to pick up the sacks (1¼ hundredweight each) and load them onto my own trailer, and then I had to manhandle them all again when I got them to the buildings. After that back-breaking exercise I decided it was time we had a road across the field. I paid an early call on the landlord, but before I could put forward a proposal I had in mind, he curtly pointed out that, as all my predecessors had managed quite well without a road, why could I not do the same? However, when I explained that I was prepared to meet the cost, his objections melted away and I was given permission to go ahead.

Following the example of my father and grandfather, who had encountered similar difficulties in their day, I took a spade and, beginning at the roadside, took off the top-soil to about a foot in depth, and eight to ten feet wide. From the roadside to the farmyard gate was about 200 yards. After my first hour at the job, that gate looked to be two miles away; but one yard, and then another yard, and I got there in the end. The hardcore, delivered by a local contractor, I levelled with a shovel, placing the larger stones in position by hand, like laying crazy paving. The stones were covered to a depth of three or four inches with coke clinker, also spread and levelled by hand – and there was our road.

The net cost was £70, reckoning nothing for my sweat and

toil, but when the driver of the milk-collecting lorry volunteered to drive across and pick up the milk at the dairy, and we were able to drive the car to the door instead of having to leave it at the roadside, I remembered that nothing worthwhile is achieved without effort.

When John Clementson left us rather unexpectedly, the rural dean and churchwardens of both churches did their best to maintain regular services. The Revd John had held an evening service (Evening Prayer, Evensong – what's in a name?) at both churches, one at six o'clock, the other at seven. I found all the churchwardens and other officials helpful and encouraging. St Leonard's, Priors Marston, presented me with a cheque for £3.16s.6d., being the collections taken in church on Whit Sunday, and I was deeply touched by the warm letter of appreciation from the parochial church council, dated 24 July 1949, which accompanied the cheque.

A new vicar was eventually appointed and at the service of institution and induction was 'presented' to the bishop by the patron of the livings, Earl Spencer. We had several such services over the space of a few years, and at one held in St Mary's Church, Priors Hardwick, the then Earl Spencer offered several people, including some children, a lift in his car from the church to the schoolroom, where a reception to welcome the new vicar and his wife was being held. Those favoured by Earl Spencer's invitation seemed neither surprised nor impressed – they just piled into his car. You would have thought they were accustomed to hitch-hiking and hobnobbing with earls and such every day of the week.

Our new man, the Revd Sidney Streatfeild, was an elderly married man recently returned from India. Like so many, he succeeded in getting off on the wrong foot. While his predecessor had shocked the Nonconformists, Sidney started by upsetting his own crew – his organist and choir, and before he'd been in the place long enough to know his way to the post office, he had a mutiny on his hands.

The small pipe organ was situated in the chancel, where, to the eye of a newcomer, it stuck out like a sore thumb, so the vicar decided to move it to the back of the church. The local carpenter, with the assistance of some stalwart volunteers, manhandled the organ to its new position at the back of the church after the vicar had carefully removed and numbered the pipes.

The organ had always been in the chancel, only a few feet from the choir, and they were afraid that, from the back of the church, a time lag in the sound reaching them would have a detrimental effect on the singing, and there would also be a lack of contact between organ and choir. That the vicar should act without consultation and before he'd got to know the people was a sure way of arousing antagonism. On hearing what had happened to the organ, the choir and organist immediately informed the vicar that they were on strike and would not be taking part in the services on the forthcoming Sunday, the occasion of the Harvest Festival. The poor vicar, aiming to circumvent the mutineers, asked me if I would play the organ – everybody would know the hymns, he pointed out, and the choir would not be missed. When I declined the pleasure of becoming involved, he lost his temper and said I was letting him down – or, to use his own expression, 'ratting on him'.

The very next day, strong men humped the organ back to its home in the chancel, and at the well-attended Harvest Festival services the choir and organist gave of their best. By the time Sunday came round again, life had returned to normal, and the organ had settled down comfortably in its corner in the chancel, where it took up nearly half the length of the communion rails. We didn't quite make the Sunday papers.

Reg left school in 1949, his ambition, as unswerving as ever, to become a cow-keeper. I could not afford to employ him, so he went to work on an adjoining farm – over 300 acres, with arable, sheep, beef and a few sucklers but no dairy herd. From his wages he had soon saved enough money to buy an 8-week-old weaner pig, thus starting his own stock-keeping, as his father, grandfather and great-grandfather had, with the ever-useful pig. Besides pigs, he kept poultry and bees and a few years later bought half a dozen breeding ewes and ran them with mine. At weekends, Saturday night and Sunday, he often did maintenance work on the railway.

In his early twenties he married a farmer's daughter who had worked on a farm from the day she left school and who shared his interest and his ambition. He then applied for a Warwickshire County Council smallholding.

Warwickshire has been in the smallholdings business eighty years and owns or rents holdings all over the county, nearly a hundred in all. The first farm purchased for chopping up into smallholdings was of 200 acres, near Priors Marston, and one of the holdings adjoined our farm on the opposite side to that of our 300-acre neighbour. With such a large number of farms in their possession, farms became vacant at fairly regular intervals, and Reg was optimistic. He was 'long-listed' from time to time, and he and his wife were invited to 'walk' a farm and inspect the house and buildings, but nothing came of these invitations, and five years passed without a tenancy's being offered him. Still hopeful, he waited and viewed more holdings, but another five years passed and nothing came his way, and he began to think that perhaps his tie was not the right colour or that a 'back-hander' in the right place might do the trick.

In desperation, he applied for a holding in two other counties, Leicestershire and Buckinghamshire, and to his astonishment was short-listed, approved and offered a tenancy in both within a few months. For various reasons he decided to emigrate to Buckinghamshire to take on a run-down farm. The rent was low because of its condition, but he and his wife began improving it and, as they had planned, set about building up a pedigree herd of Friesian dairy cows. At the end of three years the smallholdings committee offered him a larger farm with refurbished house and modern buildings.

Difficult though it was for a young man to get into a smallholding in the sixties, it was ten times more difficult in the eighties, and milk quotas have made things even worse. A farmer's son, approved as a tenant to take over from his father when he retires, is a lucky man. A young man coming into farming from outside would need a millionaire for a father – the cost of financing even a small farm would be quite beyond the means of most young hopefuls, even with family help.

Of the students at agricultural colleges, some are farmers'

sons preparing to go home and instruct the 'old man' on how he should run his farm; others hope to obtain posts as farm managers or technical advisers, while only a very few expect to buy or rent a farm, and they are either very rich or very stupid – stupid because, if not rich, they will need to borrow heavily, and that is a sure way of courting disaster.

Between the wars, many villagers with full or part-time jobs rented a field or two on which were kept a cow, some sheep, a few poultry and perhaps a breeding sow. The postman whose holding we took over was a typical example. The roadman too rented some roadside fields in which he grazed sheep and bullocks. It was quite surprising how neatly edged was the road running alongside his fields, and the grass verges supplied him with a few loads of cheap hay. These part-timers obtained pleasure and satisfaction, as well as a worthwhile profit, from their hobby, and asked nothing more of life than to be allowed to spend evenings and weekends on their 'bit o' land'.

For some, their small-scale, part-time activities were the bottom rung of a ladder up which, by hard work, thrift and determination, they were able to rise and become full-time farmers.

As soon as possible after the war, we began building up the poultry flock again, but instead of breeding our own replacements we bought day-old pullets from a hatchery in Yorkshire, which we collected from the nearest railway station. In cold weather we would find them chirping sleepily in their boxes near the fire in the station-master's office.

We carried the eggs to the roadside once a week for collection by an egg-packing company, and almost every farmer – and many other villagers too – put out a box or two of eggs. But the time came when we discovered that packing-station prices showed little profit, and the small egg-producer gave up the struggle and disappeared from the scene. Present-day 'farm gate' sales of free-range and deep-litter eggs are but a remnant of what was once a widespread, fascinating and profitable sideline for many country folk. The much-criticized battery cage, made possible by the arrival of electricity in rural areas, gave the signal for 'big business' to muscle in, and soon large-scale eggs- and broiler-production swung into action.

One day in the early fifties, an attractive young lady in a clean white coat turned up and took a sample of water from the well. Shortly afterwards we were notified that our water was impure and quite unsatisfactory for cooling milk, and that without a pure supply our licence to produce milk would be revoked. Presumably the water was pure enough for us and our young family to drink.

I wrote to the Agricultural Executive Committee (AEC), explaining our predicament, and received a visit from two bigwigs who, after carefully inspecting the premises, had a long chat with the landlord. Soon afterwards we were connected to a private supply fed by a spring – a public mains supply was not available. Cattle drinking-troughs were then placed in the fields, a new dairy was built, the old cowshed gutted and fitted out with tubular steel stanchions, water piped into the kitchen, and a lovely brass tap fitted above the old brown glazed sink.

Our farmer-landlord, a bricklayer and all-round handyman in his younger days, did all the skilled work himself, while I served him as 'labourer' – carrying bricks and mixing concrete. He was a good workman, and the buildings were approved for the production of Tuberculin Tested (TT) milk. For these improvements I paid the landlord six per cent interest on his capital outlay. This had amounted to £100 pounds and meant an additional £6 per annum on the rent. We were both well satisfied.

The buildings now complied with the regulations governing the production of milk, but when I went out of the house on dark winter mornings with only a smoky oil lamp to light my way, and if a gust of wind blew it out when I turned the corner of the house, I groped my way to the cowshed in the dark before attempting to relight it. The arrival of electricity a year or so later, with its electric motors, buttons and switches, brought us into the modern world.

Milk-production still provided the major part of the income of many small farmers in the early sixties and continued to do so until the introduction of the bulk milk tank, or vat. The installation of these vats was impracticable on many farms, and when buildings needed to be adapted or a road improved, the cost was often prohibitive and the farmer simply gave up. The roadside milk churn vanished overnight, and with it went the small dairy farmer.

Electricity made possible the milking-parlour, the vat and the refrigeration of milk in bulk, and farmers able to afford these facilities began stepping up production, farmers with one hundred cows planning to increase their herds to 200, 300 and more. While half a dozen farmers in a parish might have produced 200 gallons a day between them, they were replaced by one farmer producing 500 gallons a day – the expensive buildings required being erected with the aid of a substantial grant.

Though hundreds of small producers were put out of business, large-scale production was encouraged. Eventually quotas became necessary to stem the flood of milk and to discourage the cupidity of the big man determined to become bigger still, whatever the consequences.

No government, in Britain or on the Continent, seems to possess the courage to use the one really effective weapon against over-production – a drastic reduction in the price of the product.

Before I had been many months in the preaching business, I realized that my qualifications, to say nothing of my general education were inadequate. Among my fellow readers (all male, of course, at that time) were teachers, doctors, solicitors and their like, and though they were as nice a bunch of fellows as you were likely to meet in a month of Sundays, at any gathering of the fraternity I couldn't help wondering how I, a swede-chomping yokel, came to be in their company.

I had a word with the warden, Canon H.W. Baines (rector of Rugby), who informed me that a course of post-admission studies was available to readers, consisting of five written examinations and a thesis, the laurel awarded for successful completion being an 'Archbishops' Diploma for Readers'. He said he couldn't possibly spare the time to coach me himself but thought that a curate of his, a Mr Tompkins, who had done some post-graduate teaching at Cambridge, might be persuaded to take me on.

The Revd John Tompkins was willing, so after completing my morning business at the cattle market, where I might have sold lambs, bought a cow or ordered cattle-feed, I spent an hour in his study while Annie did her shopping. Eggs were still scarce in those days, so I usually left a dozen at the rectory and took a few for Mr Tompkins.

Most weeks I was set an essay to write, and the following week we went through it together, my tutor's criticism all but tearing it to shreds. He sometimes sat on the hearthrug while we discussed some knotty point of doctrine and drank the coffee his landlady had brought in for us.

I succeeded in passing three of the five exams in two years, collecting one certificate along the way, but when work for the next autumn examination came up for discussion, I knew I would not be able to devote sufficient time to study during the preceding busy summer months, so I decided not to enter for it, and when my tutor left Rugby to take up an appointment as chaplain and assistant master at Eton, I gave up the idea of further study. Nevertheless, I regarded my 'one to one' experience of tutorial as a privilege, though it was sometimes rather irksome, and I'm sure my fellow farmers would have said that I needed my head 'looking at'; I must confess, there were times when I thought so too.

Unfortunately a farm is not the easiest place for a farmer to get away from when he hopes to get to church on time. I was ready to set off one Sunday evening to take a service when one of the children came running in with the news that our ewes and lambs were in a neighbour's corn. They could not be left there so we took Rover, the collie, and went off to get them back, but they had found a field of young green wheat and were most reluctant to leave it. We eventually succeeded in returning them to their own field, but I had managed to collect a couple of nasty rents in my trousers caused by the barbed wire I had clambered over, and spiteful thorns and briars had also had a go at my 'best suit'. I arrived at the church only a minute or so late, still wearing my badly torn trousers, but once I had donned cassock and surplice all was hidden from the public gaze. As the parsons say, 'A cassock can, and sometimes does, hide a multitude of sins.'

16

In the bleak midwinter

One summer evening, around 1950, I was busy in the hayfield when a parson I had never set eyes on before came across the field to me. He introduced himself as the vicar of Helidon and said I had taken services in his church when he had been on holiday, so, of course, we had never met, but that he would like me to preach in his church when he was present. I did not know what to make of him or his request, but after a word with my vicar, who had arranged the previous services, a date was arranged and I went along. The village of Helidon, about two miles from Priors Marston, is in Northamptonshire and in the diocese of Peterborough.

The pleasant, bespectacled little man insisted on preceding me out of the vestry at the beginning of the service, escorted me inside the communion rails and deferentially bowed me into the 'bishop's chair'. 'Pretend you're a bishop for once,' he said, and then turned and walked to his desk in the chancel. Later in the service he escorted me to the foot of the pulpit in the same way. Eccentric he might have been, but the VIP treatment he gave me was quite a tonic and did my ego no end of good – or did it?

His Majesty King George VI died on 6 February 1952, and the Revd S.F. Streatfield, vicar of Priors Hardwick and Priors Marston, died a few days later, following a short illness. His funeral took place the day before a united memorial service for His Majesty was to be held. The poor churchwardens were in a panic. At Mr Streatfeild's funeral they suggested to

154

the rural dean, who along with the archdeacon had conducted the service, that the royal memorial service to be held the next day should be conducted by the Nonconformist ministers. At the suggestion of a Nonconformist's conducting a service in a parish church, the rural dean, Canon Francis Aylwin, vicar of Napton, nearly had a fit. Almost breathing fire, he retorted, 'Most certainly not.' Turning to me, he said, 'You're in charge, Ray. You have the bishop's licence to officiate in church; these other gentlemen do not. You may carry on and hold the service if you wish, or you may cancel it. It's entirely up to you. Personally, I think you should cancel it. Don't you agree, Archdeacon?' That gentleman, obviously not wishing to be drawn, made some evasive remark in reply and turned away, probably as surprised as the churchwardens at the rural dean's harsh rejection of the Nonconformist fraternity.

This was a tricky situation for a young hayseed to deal with, but I knew that Mr Streatfeild would not have wished the service to be cancelled. I also knew that he had been on good terms with the Methodists and the Moravians in the parish, so I suggested that the service should go ahead, despite the rural dean's remarks, and the churchwardens agreed. The Moravian minister preached the sermon, and the Methodist circuit minister from Daventry led the prayers and read an appropriate lesson. The final hymn was to have been 'Abide with Me', but I couldn't help thinking about the vicar, who should have been taking part in the service. With this thought in mind, I took it upon myself to delete the old favourite from the hymn list and to substitute one which I hoped was equally suitable. At the end of the service Methodists, Moravians and Anglicans joined in singing 'For *all* the saints who from their labours rest'.

During the late sixties and early seventies we milked around twenty cows and reared a number of followers (young heifers to replace culled cows, and a few bullocks for fattening), but to provide sufficient hay and grass for them all on our limited acreage we found it necessary to dress the pastures with fertilizer containing a high percentage of nitrogen. The results were very satisfactory. Hay crops were heavy, and the milkers grazed lush, dark-green grass behind an electric fence, moved twice daily. Milk yields were good, and with the help of the annual price review we made a living.

Fertilizing with nitrogen was not a new thing. When we took our fields of glebe, twenty years earlier, the grass was thin and hay crops were light, so we dressed them with sulphate of ammonia. In those days it came in two-hundredweight hessian sacks. We dotted these about the field and broadcast the fertilizer by hand from buckets which we refilled from the most convenient sack. Dressings were light compared with those made later to silage crops and to grass for strip and paddock grazing. For continuous heavy grazing, fertilizer is applied at intervals throughout the summer.

Grass responded wonderfully to heavy dressing of nitrogen but, as we discovered, it spelt death to some of the rarest and most beautiful wild flowers, and some of the finer grasses also disappeared. One spring, no purple orchids greeted us in pastures where they had once bloomed abundantly and regularly. At first we were not too concerned about the disappearance of a few flowers, but later we missed them and felt quite guilty, realizing that we might never see them again and that, while it was easy enough to destroy these beautiful flowers, it was impossible to replace them.

Then, to our dismay, the cowslips vanished. One six-acre meadow had been yellow and fragrant with them as long as the oldest member of the clan could remember – indeed, April hardly seemed like April without them. One thing was certain: 'Six-acre' would no longer be known as 'the cowslip field', and a 'drop o' cowslip' would be as scarce as nuts in May.

In the past, women from the villages, and some men too, had raided the meadows every year, filling large baskets with deliciously scented cowslip heads, all destined to be transformed into heart-warming amber liquid, yet however savagely the fields were plundered, the following year's crop of flowers was unaffected. If it is true that the removal of flowerheads encourages a plant to produce more blooms the next time round, the cowslip-pickers were working in harmony with nature, while I and my fertilizer most certainly were not.

Cowslip wine was regarded as the champagne of

home-mades, and though some might say they preferred elderberry, others that nothing could touch parsnip, a bottle of well-matured cowslip was the nectar brought out for a special occasion or for the special guest.

The death of our vicar left the rural dean and churchwardens with an unexpected interregnum on their hands, and at a very difficult time of year – Lent, with Easter on the horizon, so they sent me out to hunt up any retired clergy who might have settled in surrounding villages.

During the ministry of John Clementson, who was good at finding 'special preachers', the vicar of a very small parish in Northamptonshire often came to preach, so I went to see him. I found him sitting outside his front door, and I could see at a glance that he was not the same man we had previously known. When I got round to telling him the purpose of my errand, a few tears began to trickle down his cheek. I was surprised and a little disturbed and suddenly wished I hadn't called – it was very obvious that he wasn't himself.

Then he took my hand and said, in a broken voice, 'I've been a failure here, Barrett. I'm a failure.'

Completely lost for words for a moment, I then chatted on about the services we had in mind, and gradually the old fellow brightened up and promised to come and preach if we would collect him. He was a Cambridge MA, with a deep but lively interest in philosophy – once he was up in the pulpit, you never knew when he was coming down. Not the best man, perhaps, to preach to a congregation of fewer than half a dozen country folk, but as to his being a failure, who could possibly be the judge of that?

Our new vicar, the Revd Meredith Lewis, was an active man and arranged his services so that he rarely had need of my help, but I was found plenty to do in other parishes in the south of the diocese. The assistant bishop of Coventry, the Rt. Revd William Newnham-Davis, enjoyed the living of Ladbroke, a village on the A423 near Southam, and I frequently took services there while the bishop was fulfilling his duties elsewhere.

Parsons call at the most inconvenient times. Mr Lewis

drove into the yard one morning while I was cleaning out the cowsheds, my 'wellies' thickly coated with the real smelly stuff. He said he had been asked to enquire whether I still had any thoughts about being trained for the ministry. I had to admit that I had never given the idea a passing thought for many years. Since I hadn't mentioned it to him or to his predecessor, I was both puzzled and surprised, but he soon enlightened me.

He explained that at the last monthly get-together of the deanery clergy – deanery chapter, I think they call it – he had been chatting with the rural dean and the assistant bishop about my work and background. The outcome of their little chat was that, if I still wished to offer myself as a candidate for the ministry, all three – vicar, rural dean and assistant bishop – would accompany me and introduce me to the bishop as a suitable candidate for ordination.

Needless to say, I was quite overwhelmed by such an unusual and unexpected suggestion, but I promised to think it over and, of course, to discuss it with my wife. Annie was not too keen but said that the decision rested with me. We both got on splendidly with the Aylwins, and Mrs Aylwin, who had no children of her own, made quite a fuss of our children. After much thought I decided that I had no call to the priesthood. My free spirit would have rebelled at being shackled by orthodox Anglicanism, and I had no desire to commit perjury. Though the decision was hard to make at the time, it was one I have never regretted. I would have made a rotten parson anyhow.

The heavy snowfall of the winter of 1947, besides finding its way into the record books, buried our road to the village under several feet of snow, and no motor vehicles could get through. Our neighbour, on his tall, long-legged horse, collected mail and bread for the group of farms along the road. As soon as snow stopped falling, we mustered a gang and set about clearing a way through to the village.

After most of the snow had gone, severe gales uprooted a number of elm trees and left them lying right across the road, and once again we were cut off for more than a week. A few stained strips of snow persisted on the hills around us until early April.

However, the snow of 1947 was little more than a nuisance compared with the exceptionally severe frost of 1962 – 3. The frost made life difficult for us and the livestock, and it brought starvation and death to many wild birds. All drinking-troughs, indoors and out, were frozen solid, so I took an axe and chopped away the ice across the mouth of the pond, and to this I drove the cattle, including the milking cows, twice daily. For domestic needs we resorted once again to the well, extracting the water in the time-honoured method – a bucket on the end of a rope. The pipes to the house were frozen somewhere underground, and they remained frozen until the thaw relieved them.

Dozens of birds came into the cowshed at different times during the day in search of food. A few robins, blackbirds, sparrows, starlings, wrens and tits came, and most days a solitary thrush put in an appearance. Numbers decreased as the severe weather persisted, and before long, of the wrens only one was coming. For a few days the little creature, its feathers ruffled, moved disconsolately around, desperately seeking food. I wished I could help, but there was nothing I could do. The doomed little creature would fall asleep during the night, and daybreak would fail to rouse it. Following that terrible winter, it was several years before the wren's cheery song was heard again in our locality.

One spring day I noticed a small bird running backwards and forwards near the front door of a recently built house. I took it to be a sparrow amusing itself in the spring sunshine, but after a second glance I could see that the bird, somewhat larger than a sparrow was, in fact, a skylark – a bird of the wide, open spaces – and I wondered what it was doing so near an occupied dwelling. My curiosity aroused, I remained at a distance and watched. I saw it run backwards and forwards a number of times, a distance of five or six feet, and then hop onto the doorstep of the house, pause a moment, look around in a somewhat puzzled manner and then repeat very much the same exercise all over again. Sometimes it would run round and round, almost in a circle instead of backwards and forwards. The bird probably knew what it was doing, but I was very puzzled.

Since I am not a skylark or a naturalist, my attempts at solving the riddle were little more than guesswork. The house had been built during the winter on a site in the corner of a cornfield, now down to grass. It was possible that the house and roadway had been built over the lark's former nesting-site and that it had succeeded in some wonderful way – 'unerring instinct', it might be called – in locating the exact spot, though now buried under a foot of concrete. Unfortunately the lark could not explain its strange behaviour and obvious distress, while I could only guess – and offer it my sympathy.

In 1957 Canon Frank Aylwin, vicar of Napton, collapsed and died outside the church one Sunday morning on his way home after conducting Matins. His remains, along with those of his wife, lie a few feet from the chancel door of the church of St Lawrence, in the parish he served faithfully for thirty years.

He was succeeded by the Revd Claude Sparshott, who stayed nine years. I had duties in other parishes and never met the gentleman, but I know he was involved in a spot of trouble that arose about goings-on in the churchyard. Gravestones were being moved to make machine mowing easier. This has been done in many places, the stones being placed round the perimeter of the churchyard, but in Napton some of the gravestones were carted away, broken up and used as hardcore for the base of a driveway being laid at a property in the village. One or two families, on hearing that their ancestors' gravestones had been smashed up, got quite excited, accusing the vicar of sacrilege, and worse. How far he was personally responsible for this act of vandalism no one seemed to know; he probably had no idea that the men sent to move the stones would take them out of the churchyard. But whether he was innocent or guilty of personal involvement, most parishioners held him responsible for what had happened, and so he found himself 'carrying the can' and somewhat less popular for a while.

Since the day, over thirty years ago, when I stood leaning on my muck-fork while the vicar tried to measure me for a dog-collar, the Church, like farming has undergone change. We are reminded almost daily that we live in a changing world and that the Church must change with it. Certainly revision of the Book of Common Prayer was long overdue, although the Alternative Service Book (ASB) is a real curate's egg.

The book includes an alternative form of banns of marriage, and it concludes like this: 'If any of you know any reason in law why these persons should not marry, you are to declare it, now.' This ugly, formal concoction of words sounds like something being read out by the clerk in a magistrates' court, and no hint is given of the religious significance of a wedding in church.

People are 'married' in a register office or other place licensed for the purpose. In church, besides being married in the eyes of the law, they are also 'joined together in holy matrimony' following sacred vows made in the sight of God and the congregation. A wedding is a very serious business – a happy occasion, of course, but not one to be taken lightly. Indeed, in the Book of Common Prayer the marriage service bears the title 'Solemnization of Matrimony'.

The traditional form of banns is a beautifully worded reminder, surely more necessary these days than ever before, that at the marriage service couples exchange sacred vows. Being 'joined together in holy matrimony' in church means much more than simply 'getting married' and complying with the law of the land.

Of the spate of new translations of the Bible churned out in recent years, one, the *New English Bible*, hailed in a blaze of publicity as the achievement of the age, was soon found to be an unworthy successor of the Authorized Version for use in churches. We are at liberty to read what we choose in our own homes, and students and preachers obviously need to compare different versions, but for public reading in church the quality and beauty of the language are important.

An example of what scholars can accomplish when they set their minds to a task is to be found in I Corinthians 13:13. In the AV the verse begins, 'And now abideth' – three simple words replaced in the NEB by this eleven-word gem of concise writing: 'In a word, there are three things that last for ever.'

There are other lapses, but the one example should suffice to condemn it in the opinion of all who love our language. It now seems to be losing favour and might eventually follow Dr Moffat's translation into obscurity. Of the rest, one or two are wearing well, though they have yet to pass the supreme test – the test of time.

A *New English Bible* once occupied valuable space in my small bookcase, so I took it along to an Oxfam shop, and when I thought no one was looking, I popped it on a shelf and walked quietly away. Many months later I learned that Keith Waterhouse, the well-known author and columnist, had sent his *New English Bible* to a jumble sale.

Our last arable crops were harvested with a combine operated by an agricultural contractor, and when I saw the huge machine mop up in a few minutes the two acres my parents and grandparents had laboriously reaped by hand, I couldn't help wondering what they would have made of it.

Soon we were back to all pasture, but livestock require attention seven days a week throughout the year. The arable farmer can leave his fields to the hares and the larks during the winter, but for the stockman, winter is the busiest time. A couple of days at the Royal Show, which we thoroughly enjoyed, was the only break we had. Neither Annie nor I ever feel the need of a holiday.

A favourite relaxation of mine in summer was a late-evening walk round the fields. Leaning on a gate, I could study the cattle with my stockman's eye or simply stand and stare at the trees and watch the sun sink slowly from sight behind the distant hills. It was probably as good a way as any of recharging tired batteries, while the beauty around me, the quietness and the solitude were ideal for pondering over a sermon. Before me were the fields and hills, the sheep and cattle, the flowers of the fields and the birds of the air, and pools of water – all the material I could ever possibly need for all the sermons I could possibly preach in a lifetime. Unfortunately I lacked the ability to make the best use of all that lay at my feet.

On my walk one evening I caught a whiff of fragrant tobacco smoke coming from somewhere near at hand. Then I spotted my neighbour, Jo, leaning with his back against a fence, quietly smoking his pipe. I joined him, but he too must have been in reflective mood, for few words passed, except a comment about the weather, agreeing that it was 'a grand evening'. A good sheep man, Jo had one eye on his sheep and lambs, scattered over the field and grazing contentedly; his Old English sheepdog, with no interest in the sheep at that time of day, lay at his feet. Directly overhead, two stars were just visible against the evening sky.

When we did talk, the conversation somehow got round to the church and the parsons. Jo said he had been brought up Church of England but hadn't attended a service for years. He said that his terrible experiences during the '14 – 18 war, and the chaplain's preaching the duty to kill as many fellow human beings as possible, had sickened him and others too. With the bowl of his pipe in his hand and using the stem as a pointer, he stretched out his arm and described a wide arc, taking in fields, sky, sheep and trees. 'This is my church,' he said, and replaced his pipe in his mouth. I gathered from that laconic statement that he obtained from his farm some deep, inner satisfaction neither parson nor creed could give him. One thing was certain: Jo was a contented man. He lived with his stock and close to his land and seemed almost as much a part of his environment as were the sheep and the trees, all of which went to make him a very practical man.

The farmer deals with realities: birth, death, seed-time and harvest, flood, drought, blizzard and disease among crops and livestock. The land itself is a living thing and responds to the treatment and care – or lack of it – it receives from the husbandman. The genuine farmer knows his land and feels towards it as he does towards his cattle and sheep. Not so the 'agri-business' tycooon and highly paid professional consultant. A.G. Street, in his book *Coopers' Crossing*, has one character say to another, a large-scale wheat-grower, 'You do not love the land. You do not want to love it. You only want to grip it by the throat and shake money out of it.'

Britain's wheatlands have been squeezed hard for many years, and with the aid of heavy dressings of nitrogen have yielded bountiful harvests of grain, stuffing growers' coffers with gold. Only when agriculture is in a depressed state, when nobody wants land and when prices are low, is it possible to get into the farming business. For my grandson,

Tom (Jim Barrett's great-great-grandson), and for many of his contemporaries, the outlook is far from rosy as we enter the last decade of the century. A new generation will take over – it always does, but there must be no feather-bedding. The young must accept that farming is a risky business – that is why it is so fascinating. They must stand on their own feet and battle it out against the odds. Without grants and subsidies and facing an open, competitive market, the inefficient would fall by the wayside. Only the fittest would survive – and why should it not be so?

We usually baled fifteen or twenty acres of straw on a nearby farm for use during the winter, and on more than one occasion the farmer put a match to the remaining unwanted straw before we had left the field with the last load of bales. Seeing it go up in flames was something I never did get used to. There seemed to be something almost obscene in the spectacle of acres and acres of blackened stubble and smoking ashes where, an hour or two earlier, bright, crisp straw had stretched in long rows across the field. Brought up to believe that everything produced on the farm could be put to good use, I couldn't help thinking of those days of scarcity when Dad and his neighbours had travelled five or six miles sometimes more, with a horse and cart to bring home a few boltens of straw. The excuses put forward in justification of the dangerous, filthy practice of burning are plausible enough but not entirely convincing.

Yet, however much we may hate it, we have to face the fact that there is a surplus of the stuff and that it has to be disposed of. Legislation, made necessary by the conduct of the careless and irresponsible, was inevitable. Meanwhile alternative methods of dealing with the surplus are being tried out, but they are only in the experimental stage at present and cannot be expected to solve the problem quickly, and that any means of disposing of rape straw and similar rubbish, other than by setting fire to it, is unlikely. Research, experimental work and farming are long-term jobs, and the bleatings of short-sighted, impatient, publicity-seeking pressure groups cannot change that.

It is interesting to reflect on what would happen if every

vegetarian in the country suddenly decided to eat meat again. The countryside would certainly be transformed. Many acres of arable land would return to pasture to carry the extra livestock demanded. Less grain, and much less straw, would be produced, many fewer tons of chemical fertilizer used, and hedges would be needed to make stockproof fields and windbreaks. Much of the straw grown would be used to bed down the stock indoors during the winter and, as manure, would be returned to the land. More organic fertilizers would be available in the form of bonemeal, hoof- and hornmeal and dried blood – products in keen demand now that we are all clamouring for healthy, organically grown food.

When I first saw a barbecue in operation, I jumped to the conclusion that here was another toy for those with money to burn. Now I know better. Home from work on a summer afternoon, man and woman hasten to be rid of the trammels of civilization. The man strips to the waist, and the woman dons her sunsuit. Half-naked, they are ready for the flesh eating-orgy. This highly civilized, two-legged animal seizes a chicken leg in his hand and proceeds to tear off the flesh with teeth designed for the job – you can almost hear him growl as he gnaws away. His creator has supplied organs for converting meat into bone, muscle, energy and much more – and, for his delight, an appetite and a palate guaranteeing enjoyment of a juicy joint are also supplied. The call of the wild runs deep; for the sake of meat-producers, let us hope it always does.

17

Come, labour on

Stock farmers will best remember the 1960s for the foot-and-mouth disease which devastated livestock in the winter of 1967–8, when over 400,000 head of stock were slaughtered, including many valuable pedigree cattle, sheep and pigs. We turned on the radio every morning for the farming news but were almost afraid to listen as the number of outbreaks and the localities affected were announced. Gradually the dark, threatening cloud passed over and we were able to breathe again. We used the car only when it was absolutely necessary. With markets closed and movement of livestock forbidden farmers stayed at home as much as possible, nor were visitors welcome. Every possible precaution was taken to prevent the spread of infection. Though we saw a few of those heart-breaking 'funeral pyres', no pestilence came near us, and we were thankful for our deliverance.

However, stock farmers cannot escape losses altogether: they are part of the job. Over the years we were fortunate and contributed very little towards the support of the knacker-man and his family. Sometimes, when a sheep died in an outlying field, instead of carting it to the roadside for the knacker-man to collect, I dug a hole in the ground near the carcase, rolled it in and covered it with sufficient earth to ensure that dogs and foxes would not interfere with it. Prowling scavengers spread disease.

On one occasion, some months after I had buried a sheep in

this way, I noticed that the small patch of grass, marking almost exactly the area of the grave, had become a rich, dark green and was outgrowing the pale, thin grass surrounding it. This conspicuous square of grass was obviously receiving some extremely good nourishment from the putrefying carcase lying below. During its lifetime, the dead animal had obtained nourishment from the grass its decaying body was now enriching, and the grass in its turn was now providing food for other animals. Had a few lettuce seeds been sown on the spot and fenced off from animals, some crisp, crunchy, salad lettuce would have been produced, organically grown – the natural way – and greatly relished by discriminating vegetarians.

Veterinary science has made it possible to protect sheep against many serious diseases by simple, routine injections, but nothing has yet been found to protect harmless sheep against savage attacks by wandering, uncontrolled dogs. Dogs cause terrible suffering to sheep, and many are killed, sheep-worrying has compelled farmers near towns to give up keeping sheep, and in financial terms losses run into many thousands of pounds each year. Sheep-worrying is seldom a newsworthy subject unless some irate farmer has shot somebody's darling pet caught tearing one of his sheep to pieces.

In 1976 came the drought still talked about in the late eighties. That it was severe is little doubt, but at the farm we were not nearly so badly affected as we had been in the long, hot summer which occurred just after the war. The 1976 drought was not so prolonged as the earlier one, as my diary shows.

The ponds dried up, but that gave us an opportunity to have a contractor in to dredge out the mud. We had recently been connected to a mains water supply, and this kept the field troughs full. To avoid mixing together animals of different ages, I decided to take water to outlying fields. For this I needed nearly half a mile of plastic piping, two galvanized troughs and a miscellaneous collection of fittings, but the scheme worked and the cattle were never without water for a day through that hot summer of 1976. Grass became scarce and we fed some hay, but we heard none of that plaintive lowing which had distressed us so much thirty years earlier. When the rains came, the pastures regained their colour in a matter of days, as they always do. Lawns, too, recover quickly after a good soak. Experience taught us the true value of water, and we would never think of watering a lawn.

These are a few of the entries in my weather diary for that summer:

> Saturday, June 19th. Puddles in the road and overflowing rain-water tanks. Must have been a lot of rain during the night.
> August 12th [Thursday]. End of harvest. Earliest and driest season in living memory. Topic of the day – drought and acute water shortage.
> Monday, August 30th. (Late summer holiday.) Had hoped to watch a bit of cricket on TV but heavy rain at Edgbaston had soaked the ground.
> Wednesday, September 1st. Fields a little greener after the rain but not making much growth yet.

We also remember that decade for the startling rise in inflation which continued through the seventies. Farm rents rose sharply and were then reviewed every three years. The rent of our two glebe fields, £24 per annum in 1939, had risen to £200 in 1979, and the rent of the 43-acre holding had risen from £55 to £900. Farm workers' wages rose from 35 shillings a week to £70 over the same period. But of course farm prices rose too. Dairy cows could still be bought for around £50 after the war (1950) but by 1980 had risen to over £500. Definitely a seller's market.

When I was sent to take evening service at Napton one Sunday while the vicar was on holiday, I was surprised to see that one of the bookcases at the back of the church contained a number of Methodist hymn-books. A sidesman explained that the Methodist church was closed, but one Sunday a month, when the vicar had a service in another parish, the Methodists 'borrowed' the parish church and held a service there, the church organist and choir turning up to lead the singing. Methodism was being kept alive in Napton with the aid and co-operation of the vicar, church officers and staff of the parish church.

A short time before the service was due to begin, a group of about half a dozen ladies trooped in, boosting the congregation by nearly one hundred per cent. They noticed the Methodist hymn-books, were obviously surprised to see them there and were delighted to learn of the church's gesture. They said they were Methodists on a canal-boating holiday and had tied up at Napton for the night. Their leader explained that over a number of years they had found so many Methodist chapels closed that they now regularly made for the Anglican church, which was usually easy to find, and they had also grown to like the service. As they left the church, the same good lady thanked me for a 'very beautiful service'. I began to preen myself and waited for her to compliment me on my stirring sermon; instead, she said they were deeply impressed by the Prayer Book service – it seemed to have a 'timeless beauty' about it. Little did she know that at that very time learned men were in a huddle concocting something destined to call 'time' on that 'timeless beauty'.

Around the end of August 1978 the organist from Napton church came to see me. She said she had the chance of a holiday – a once-in-a-lifetime opportunity for a tour of the Holy Land, and would I play the organ for her on the two Sundays she would be away? I said I was free and would be pleased to help her out. At choir practice I learned that on one of those Sundays I would be playing for the Methodist monthly service. There were no tricky chants to play but the hymns were unfamiliar to me, and not nearly as lively and singable as I had expected. When I turned over the pages of my book of voluntaries, I was surprised to see that I had written in the margin underneath one voluntary, 'Napton church, August 18th. 1927.' Alongside that I wrote, 'Napton church, September 10th. 1978.' How time does fly. In my diary for that day I wrote, 'My day at the organ here was a nostalgic occasion loaded with memories, particularly so since many of those who worshipped there then are now only names on gravestones I passed on my way into church.'

Two of the graves I passed were those of Dad and Mother.

Dad had been confined to his bed for three or four years when Mother died at the age of seventy-five. He continued to take an active interest in the farm business and church affairs for some years after her death. He died in 1961 aged eighty-eight.

Fortunately, they did not have to leave the farm when health failed them. They occupied rooms in part of the house while Vic, married and with a family, took charge of the farm, including the rented land, and occupied the remainder of the house. Although buying the house had been a struggle for Tom and Maggie they were rewarded by being able to spend their last days in familiar surroundings with their family around them.

In October our vicar, the Revd David Broadbent, retired and left the parish. On his appointment he had been given charge of Wormleighton, a third parish added to the two Priors but all three under the patronage of Earl Spencer, whose family are landlords of many acres of land in all three parishes. We now had three churches needing a regular rota of services, but with another reader now living in Priors Marston and retired clergy willing to help, things went smoothly.

One glorious Sunday evening I was taking the service in Priors Marston church, the door standing wide open, when, over half way through the service, a group of four, possibly five, young people clumped noisily into the church, two of them with guitars slung on their backs. Having no idea who they were, I was afraid they intended disrupting the service, but they behaved impeccably. After the service they told us they were on a boating tour on the canal – a working holiday. They said they were a 'gospel' group from the mid-Western states of America. They sang, read the Bible and preached on canal wharves and in market squares, shopping centres and other likely places. We asked them if they would sing a few of their songs for us before they left, and they readily agreed: standing on the chancel steps they entertained us with some lively singing. The walls of St Leonard's Church had heard nothing like it before, although we did regard ourselves as being in step with the times – indeed, that very evening our lessons had been read, one from the *Good News Bible*, the other, from the *Jerusalem Bible*. As they were leaving, some inquisitive member of our company asked them which version of the Bible they used, and the young man carrying a leather-bound Bible in his hand held it above his head and replied, 'Good King James,' of course.

That we should be without a vicar for some time dawned on us when we were informed that the vicarage had been sold and that no appointment would be made until a new one had been built. Things got moving without too much delay, but then, when we thought we might soon be hearing news of a new vicar, we learned that Earl Spencer was seriously ill. The patron of the living usually has some say in the appointment of an incumbent, but in certain circumstances, the bishop may act alone and proceed to fill a vacancy. Countess Spencer disliked this idea. She said her husband was recovering and expected to be able to take his part in the selection of an incumbent, and to present him to the bishop at the service of 'Institution'. Thanks largely to Countess Spencer's devoted nursing, Earl Spencer did make a full recovery in time to fulfil his duties as a conscientious patron.

The Spencer family has been associated with Wormleighton for centuries. The manor there was the family home until they moved to Althorp.

On my last visit to the Royal Show I walked round acres and acres of giant-sized, gaudily painted machines, the whole dazzling array proclaiming the designers' inventiveness and the engineers' skill. It was difficult to believe that most of those brightly coloured monsters were made to perform the same basic operations as did my grandparents' primitive tools – to plough and sow, reap and mow, and do a bit of muck-spreading.

The farmer rubbing out an ear of corn in the palm of his hand, his eyes anxiously scanning the sky; the shepherd cleaning the nose and mouth of a newly born lamb with his finger, and hearing its first faint bleat – these things are the centre and purpose of it all. No machine can do these things, yet around them all the rest revolve. Opportunities for our young men and women to learn and develop these ancient skills exist in colleges and elsewhere but, unfortunately for most of them, farms of their own on which to put those skills into practice will never be more than a dream.

There is irony in the fact that, though arable farmers are being paid to 'set-aside' (i.e. not crop) a percentage of their land, small farms urgently needed by would-be young farmers are still, being swallowed up at an alarming rate.

In 1964 250,000 farmers succeeded in getting a living off farms of less than a hundred acres; by the early eighties the number had dwindled to 120,000. I mentioned earlier that getting into farming is prohibitively expensive and that the young hopeful would need a millionaire for a father; if the present trend of vanishing farms continues, the richest of fathers would also need a magic wand.

Napton-on-the Hill still has its school, though only a 'first school'. On the wall facing the road are two tablets, each inscribed with a biblical text. One is from Proverbs 22: 6 – 'Train up a child in the way he should go: and when he is old, he will not depart from it.' The second is from one of St Paul's epistles, though I do not remember which. From time to time ivy creeps up the wall and obscures these scriptural admonitions, but as regularly it is cut back and the texts revealed for all to see.

And there is talk of filling in the roadside pond at the bottom of the village, now overgrown and neglected. We, in our day, rolled up our sleeves, took spades and shovels and cleaned it out. Though we may have appreciated it mainly for its usefulness, today, if conservation means anything, it should surely be appreciated and preserved for its aesthetic value and for its importance to small wild-life that once abounded in and around it. Some years ago, because the surrounding fence was considered unsafe, the ducking pond was filled in. Thus, almost unnoticed, do bits of our local history disappear for ever.

As in other villages, house-builders have been much too busy. Paddocks, orchards and other attractive plots of green have nearly all disappeared under bricks and mortar. These islands of green turf give the village its character and that much-appreciated 'openness' we all expect to find in any village, large or small. 'Infilling', if it is allowed to continue unchecked, will turn many of our beautiful villages into ugly, miniature towns. An old Naptonian I spoke to in the churchyard made the laconic comment, 'Money talks, and they get away with it.'

Since that pithy remark was made, county structure plans have been falling like bombs, and many rural communities are reeling with dismay. In Napton, several large plots of land in and around the village are marked as possible sites for future development. People moving into these 'exclusive developments', as they are likely to be called, would presumably work in town, and in the absence of public transport they would need cars – some families, more than one. For some years after the war half a dozen buses ferried people to and from Coventry and Leamington; now a stream of cars, many containing only the driver, jam the roads and foul the air, and the nuisance could only get worse when more people with even more cars moved in from outside the area.

Conservationists insist that some means of controlling the noxious, four-wheeled animal must be found before it is too late. Incidentally, Sir Winston Churchill said that the introduction of the internal combustion engine marked 'a very gloomy milestone in the progress of mankind'.

When the time came for us to retire, which we did with the greatest reluctance, we began looking around for somewhere to live. We looked first around our 'home' villages but found nothing we could afford. We then began hunting further and further afield, but without success. Eventually we were forced to face the truth. Being tenant farmers with no property to sell, we would not be able to afford a decent house in the country, and so we reconciled ourselves to the idea of living in town. It was something we had never contemplated – the very thought of it appalled us, but we had no choice.

Unfortunately that is the lot of many country people today. Young couples hoping to set up home together cannot possibly afford a house in their native village, or in any other village, and are forced to move into town. Retired farm and estate workers leaving their tied cottages, and small tenant farmers vacating their holdings, face the same ordeal. They have to tear themselves up by the roots, leave much-loved, familiar surroundings and life-long friends behind and try to settle down in a town. Homes for young people and for the retired are needed as urgently in the country as in the town. Developers and builders are interested only in building for the well-heeled, able to afford luxury homes. More and more people can now indulge in a second home – a weekend cottage. A young local couple looking for a home see the cottage they had set their hearts on making a ridiculous price, and then stand empty except at weekends. The chances of my being able to end my days in my native village – the playground of my childhood and the resting-place of my fathers since the seventeenth century – seem remote indeed. That there might be a place for me in the churchyard there is poor consolation.

Though Annie and I moved into town when we retired from farming, my brother, Vic, lives in the house in the village and still farms the holding Jim Barrett moved to in 1896. The twenty acres of glebe of which I became the proud tenant in 1939 were put up for sale when we relinquished the tenancy, but Reg was able to buy them for £900 per acre; he also rents other land nearby and pays a local man to tend the stock. Reg, too, hopes to return to his native acres one day, thus extending the continuity of the family's connection with farming in the area to the fourth generation; and of this intention Jim Barrett and Tom would have approved, though it would have saddened them to see the old cottage falling into ruin.

My cousin, Deric Alsop, the carrier's son and bearer of my mother's family name, is also still farming the paternal acres, with the addition of some outlying land, though a son is now the active member of the business and occupies the house from which the young man's great-grandfather started the carrying business at the turn of the century. Their income comes from a moderate-sized dairy herd.

That both sides of the family have continued to make a living from small-scale pastoral farming explodes the myth that a large acreage is needed to provide, in economists' jargon, a 'viable unit'.

A feeling of continuity, always satisfying to a farming family, is also important in village life. Residents will take an interest, perhaps pride, in a village when they feel they are a part of it – that it is the place where they belong, the place where they were born, where, like 'Gran', they hope to end their days.

Deric's other son, Mike, like my younger son, Eric James (James after old Jim), though not in farming is engaged in work closely connected with the land – making ploughs. They work in the same drawing-office at a factory not in town but deep in the Warwickshire countryside on the site of a former lime (cement) works only a stone's throw from the works where Tom found employment over a hundred years ago. It is also right beside the canal where Jim started working after his return from Canada.

In about 1970 Roger Dowdeswell, a local farmer's son, keen on machinery and with a flair for inventing, came up with what was considered a good idea, so he decided to go into business and manufacture a plough he had designed. The derelict works site was acquired and production began in earnest. Eric joined Roger in 1975 as his first draughtsman, and Mike Alsop some time later. The business prospered and grew and now has a staff of six in the drawing-office.

Ploughs and other tillage equipment are exported to many parts of the world, including the Far East. In the province of Xinjiang in north-west China twenty of their reversible ploughs are in use, while in Howlong 300 conventional Dowdeswell ploughs are working. A team from the factory travelled to China, where they instructed local workers in the operation, adjustment and maintenance of the machines.

At about the time I was putting the finishing touches to this book, Eric was in the Far East again where Dowdeswell are optimistic of doing more business. This go-ahead firm is in process of installing computers in the drawing-office – keyboard technology in operation where these young men's ancestors slogged it out with pick and shovel. But if Jim and Tom could come back and see what was happening, they wouldn't sigh for the 'old times'; they would simply say, 'Good luck to 'em. We were born a hundred years too soon, mate.'

18

All creatures of our God and King

After moving into town, I tried most of the churches within reasonable distance of home, hoping to find one in which I would feel comfortable with the type of worship practised, and with the people. I failed to find what I was seeking – perhaps I was not sure what that was. Though I was made welcome at the church I finally settled on, I felt rather lost on finding myself to be a very small fish in a very large pond, whereas for nearly forty years I had been a mighty big fish – I thought – in what I now realized had been a very small pond.

Harvest festival services in town I found very disappointing. Poorly attended, they lacked the warmth, enthusiasm and spontaneity I had always found in the country. The town no longer has any connection with agriculture or countryside, and no interest in what goes on in the fields around. What passes for bread now grows ready sliced and wrapped on supermarket shelves. A far cry from the days when Grannie plied her sickle in the harvest field and baked her bread in the faggot-heated oven. Nevertheless, I was lucky enough to get a whiff of real country air in a town church …

Before evening service at one church, two elderly priests in their cassocks stood chatting on the chancel steps, comparing each other's degree of baldness. One, with a reasonable but thinning crop, pointed to his colleague's almost bald head and remarked, 'Grass doesn't grow on barren soil.' Without batting an eyelid, the bald one retorted, 'And a sitting hen doesn't have feathers on its arse.' A few minutes later they donned their surplices and, following the choir, walked sedately to their stalls in the chancel.

Church and farm meet together at a country harvest festival, a service some clergy dismiss as semi-pagan, and it is probably true that its roots lie deep in our primitive past. Be that as it may, I was delighted to be asked to conduct a harvest festival service at Willoughby, a small village just off the A45, between Dunchurch and Daventry. When I entered the little church, I was greeted by piles of produce from field and garden, the delightful smell of mellow apples, masses of gorgeous flowers and, of course, a few sheaves of wheat. As always at a country harvest festival, the congregation sang the well-known hymns with joyful enthusiasm; rather to my surprise, they also sang the psalms and canticles with confidence.

No priest was present, so we were denied absolution and a blessing, but no one appeared to suffer as a result of the omission. Creed and dogma mean little at any time, and many people attend church only at the great festivals; nevertheless, a deep-rooted instinct prompts them to bring their gifts and offer their praises and thanksgiving to the Great Provider at harvest time as they and their ancestors have for many centuries.

Most country people are a strange mixture of agnostic, mystic and conventional, if unorthodox, Christian, yet they are probably no more 'pagan' than the poet who wrote, a few hundred years before the Christian era, 'Praise the Lord, O my soul, and forget not all his benefits.'

What makes a country church so very special, so different from most, though not all town churches, is its churchyard. It is a very haven of peace in a hurrying, noisy world – from the world it is a sanctuary. There was, in fact, a time when a fugitive could claim the right of sanctuary once he had entered the consecrated ground of the churchyard.

Naturalists and others interested in conservation have discovered that the churchyard is also a secure haven for many wild birds and small mammals. Some local flowers, once plentiful in surrounding meadows but now extinct as a result of modern farming methods, may be found hiding in the churchyard, safe from harm – until the incumbent of the parish and his aides decide to tidy up the churchyard. Gravestones are moved, mounds are levelled, rotary mowers and 'strimmers' are brought in, and volunteers then proceed to trim the whole area from hedge to hedge, or wall to wall, until it looks like a suburban garden. No one wants to see an untidy churchyard, but one in which the grass is kept short by frequent mowing and in which no wild flower dare raise its head is as hideous to the eye as a suburban front garden with its closely shaved lawn and neat rows of gaudy flowers. Though approaches and pathways need to be kept tidy, there is usually a spot, perhaps in a corner, where cutting could be postponed till late summer, when, for most creatures, the breeding-season is over for the year. In some counties, judges for the 'Best Kept Churchyard' competition now take into consideration areas left for wildlife.

Members of the Women's Institute have carried out a detailed survey of some 1,400 churchyards in England and Wales, recording valuable information about wildlife and flowers and noting any interesting details connected with each individual churchyard. Other bodies interested in churchyards are the Botanical Society of the British Isles, the British Butterfly Conservation Society and the Nature Conservancy Council; some of these organizations have carried out, or are in process of carrying out, surveys of their own.

Along with birds, flowers and butterflies in the churchyard are frogs, toads, newts, field mice and other small creatures. Those whose task it is to keep churchyards tidy should spare a thought for them. Destroyed elsewhere and with nowhere to go, they hope to find sanctuary in the quiet seclusion of the churchyard where they can live and breed without being unduly disturbed. Conservationists are merely saying: don't go mad with the mower, the 'strimmer' and the week-killer – use them sensibly.

Though the post-war corn-growing bonanza encouraged farmers to drain and plough every available square yard of ground, and led to a dramatic change in the appearance of the countryside, and harmful effects on wildlife and the environment, the truth is that changes first began to take place soon after the tractor appeared on the land over half a century ago. Farmers were not slow to appreciate that in the tractor they had at their disposal a power far exceeding that of many horses. In his book *English Social History*, published in 1941, G.M. Trevelyan wrote, 'Man is all too successfully regulating the face of nature with the machine.' Mr Trevelyan appears to have been an early and perceptive observer of what was happening as a result of the introduction of tractor power onto the land. However, following a change in government policy, pressure from conservationists, and the simple pounds and pence of it all, hedge-grubbing and pond-filling no longer yield a profit.

Incidentally, Mr Trevelyan also says in his book, 'I possess an Eighteenth Century grand-father clock, still keeping good time, which was made in the small Warwickshire village of Priors Marston.'

The country parson, like the rest of us, has come to terms with the modern world. No longer does he take tea with Miss Robinson-Smythe, who crooks her little finger divinely, nor does he collect butterflies or write books he knows no one will read. Today there are meetings, conferences, services, retreats and numerous other events he is expected to attend in the cathedral city, or even much further afield. Whether all these 'talk shops' are really necessary is doubtful, but the vicar does seem to spend a lot of time outside his parish. When he is at home, he will probably be at his desk, playing the part of an administrator rather than that of a pastor.

At the same time we ought not to expect him to spend all his time 'visiting'. While there are those who like him to drop in and are likely to complain that he is neglectful if he does not, others are less keen and are likely to call him a nosy old so-and-so if they see him coming up the garden path. Dad used to tell us about the boy happily playing in front of the house when he spotted the vicar coming down the road. Probably afraid of having his ear tweaked for being absent from Sunday School, he dashed through the house and out into the back-yard. As he shot through the kitchen he shouted, 'Look out, Mam, the bloody old parson's coming!' The sensible parson gives up trying to please everybody and grows a thick skin.

The deanery and diocesan synods have been in existence for many years, though they were known as ruridecanal and diocesan conferences in my day. At one deanery conference I attended there was the usual subdued buzz of conversation before the meeting got under way, and during this period of free-for-all chat a local cleric sitting near me was instructing those of his holy brethren within earshot, and anyone who cared to eavesdrop, how to prepare and cook a sheep's head. From none of the diocesan conferences I attended did anything nearly as interesting, or so practical, come my way. Perhaps I was asleep.

The country parson's greatest headache is, however, usually the church building, or buildings – always in need of repair or restoration. Though the same problems confront those responsible for some older town churches, the country parson may have a group of parishes in his care, one or more of them with a population of fewer than 200 souls, and these very small communities face almost insurmountable difficulties when large sums of money are required for major restoration work. Churches, like motor cars, have a limited life-span, and we happen to be living at a time when many churches are showing disturbing signs of old age and decay.

Spotlessly clean floors, shining brasswork and beautiful flowers tell of the care and attention lovingly bestowed on the church by members of the congregation in even the smallest parish. Though major restoration work is beyond the means of the faithful few, appeals are launched and set in motion – 'acts of faith', the clergy call them – and after much hard work the money is found. But it may not always be so, and the next fifty years could be crucial for many churches. Fortunately interested, far-sighted people have helped to set up trusts and invest funds for the preservation of old churches, particularly those classified as historic buildings, but more help is needed if they are to be preserved not only as examples of fine architecture but as places in which people meet together for worship.

Inside most churches a box in a prominent position invites visitors to contribute to the 'Church Restoration Fund', but now many churches are locked twenty-four hours a day during the week. The decision to lock up a church is not taken lightly, but frequent thefts, appalling acts of vandalism and advice from the police have persuaded many more incumbents to turn the key on undesirable and desirable visitors alike. The 'offertory box' no longer receives contributions from the public towards upkeep or restoration. One source of income dries up overnight.

Also barred from entry are those who love to go in and sit quietly for a while for prayer or meditation, or simply to enjoy the beauty of the building and the tranquillity to be found there. For this reason alone, many clergy are reluctant to lock their churches, which, they say, are 'houses of prayer' and should be available for private use as well as for public worship.

The most rewarding time to visit a country church is at Easter, for it is then a truly beautiful sight. No string of pious platitudes emanating from the pulpit puts across the Easter message more eloquently or more beautifully than the flowers – the lilies on the altar, the daffodils in the windows, and the primroses round the pulpit say it all. When to the message told by the flowers is added the beauty of the music, the readings and the prayers, a sermon seems superfluous, almost an intrusion.

When I tell my town friends that after living in the country I miss the birds, they think I'm mad. Here, on the outskirts of town, are birds galore: sparrows, starlings, robins, blackbirds and thrushes, tits, wrens, hedge-sparrows, finches and jackdaws, while crows and magpies also come into the garden, and a pair of fat wood-pigeons strut around the lawn as though they owned it.

Then I explain. I miss the yellowhammer droning its sleepy, monotonous song from the topmost twig of a high hedge on a hot, still summer afternoon, and I miss the heart-lifting sound of the cuckoo calling from dawn to dusk in late May and early June; but most of all I miss the lark singing overhead. I sometimes watched it climb higher and higher in the sky and then, singing as it descended until within a few feet of the ground, see it drop silently out of sight among the dark green blades of wheat.

These delightful sounds are part of the countryside and

with foresight and constant vigilance will continue to be so through the next century and beyond, despite the property developer, the road-maker and the motor car. Conservationists point out that we hold this planet in trust for those who will follow us – it is not ours to exploit, despoil or destroy.

'The earth is the Lord's, and all that therein is' – Psalm 24.1.

Index